FREEDOM
IN THE
MODERN WORLD

FREEDOM
IN THE
MODERN WORLD

By

JACQUES MARITAIN

TRANSLATED BY
RICHARD O'SULLIVAN, K.C.

GORDIAN PRESS
NEW YORK
1971

Originally Published 1936
Reprinted 1971

Published by GORDIAN PRESS, INC.
By Arrangement With
CHARLES SCRIBNER'S SONS

Library of Congress Catalog Card Number — 77-150414
ISBN 87752-147-6

CONTENTS

FOREWORD

This book derives its cohesion less from the formal treatment of a single subject than from a certain movement of thought and reflexion. This movement of thought proceeds in the discursive way of practical reason. It starts with certain general considerations in which metaphysical speculation plays a preponderating part. This gives us the first portion of the work, which is devoted to a Philosophy of Freedom. Here an effort is made to show how the universe of Freedom presupposes the universe of Nature and constitutes none the less an order apart, irreducible to that of Nature, with a dynamism that leads from an initial term of Freedom (which we call the Free Will) to a final term which may be called the Freedom of Fulfilment or of Autonomy. Important consequences follow in the realm of political philosophy, and a consideration of these consequences concludes the first part.

In the second part of the book certain themes that occupied our attention in an earlier work (*Religion and Culture*) are resumed and developed, and the thought is directed outward to facts of the historical order and to certain conditions of our time in which the major propositions already examined find room for practical application. The pursuit in this way of one leading idea gives rise to a great variety of questions that concern the notion of Order ; the opposition between authentic humanism that has God for its centre and the humanism of history that has Man for its centre ; the relations between the Spiritual and the Temporal orders ; the possible types or aspects of a new Christendom ; the temporal mission of the Christian soul ; the attitude of authentic humanism towards the existing order of civilisation ; and towards the materialism of the Capitalist and the Communist systems.

The third part of the book passes to the problem of Means (the purification or spiritual preparation of the Means) and the thought is occupied in a way proper to reflexion in the purely practical order with considerations of a concrete kind concerning lines of action that may be pursued. The matter dealt with in this last part is thrust upon the notice of the philosopher as soon as he recognises the necessity for the radical reform of a temporal order that is destructive of human personality and of true freedom ; and sees (since means must be consonant with the ends they serve) that the means to be used in such an effort of reform must be worthy of the splendour of the end in view and adequate to the renewal of the temporal order on a truly spiritual basis.

A PHILOSOPHY OF FREEDOM

A PHILOSOPHY OF FREEDOM

1. From the time of Kant and the *Critique of Practical Reason*, the opposition of Nature and of Freedom has been for modern philosophy a commonplace.

On the one hand there is the concept of Nature entirely unrelated to Ethics, an infinite concatenation of phenomena subject to the rule of determinism or absolute necessity. If our intellect terminates at a system of sensible appearances that are related and are to be interpreted on mathematical principles, and is without power to penetrate to the heart of things with a metaphysical view of their core and being and transcendental structure, what can it discover save a multitude of connexions in the phenomenal order, connexions that are more or less constructions of our thought and that are more or less deducible by mathematical processes, but that constitute what we may call a panorama of pure fact, entirely foreign to any consideration of Right or of ruling Law ?

On the other hand, the order of Ethics and of Conscience, of Good and Evil for Man, cannot but be absolutely separate from the order of Nature. It is founded exclusively on a concept of Freedom which in the thought of Kant again belonged to a system of absolute values and of beliefs or postulates

3

of the supra-sensible order, but which had to be affirmed as existing, of itself and apart, out of relation with Nature. Mankind has had occasion since the time of Kant to observe how uncertain and even precarious is the situation of Ethics if it is put on such a basis.

However that may be, it would seem either that there is no order of Freedom and of Right, or else that it exists independently of the order of Nature and of Fact and in opposition to this Order. Any contact with Nature would in sooth defile Ethics with the taint of Eudaemonism.

And yet modern philosophers are of opinion that a *Philosophy of Freedom* like a Philosophy of Mind or Spirit could only take shape after the advent of Idealism.

Our purpose in this essay is to show briefly that the philosophy of St. Thomas is not only a philosophy of Nature or, more generally, of *Being*, but that it is also, and particularly from the angle of Ethics, a *Philosophy of Freedom :* as, from the angle of Knowledge, it is a *Philosophy of Mind or Spirit ;* a philosophy too of Freedom and a philosophy of Mind or Spirit that connect one with another to a point of ultimate convergence.

But in place of opposing the order of Freedom to the order of Nature or of Being, the philosophy of St. Thomas unites without confusing them, and grounds the former on the latter.

Hegel as we know (it is his special glory) sought to overcome the Kantian disjunction of Nature and Freedom, of Fact and Law, but his inspired effort led only to their identification.

4

For St. Thomas, on the other hand, these two orders though related are always distinct.

Following the principles of his philosophy we accordingly seek to show :

(1) How the order of Freedom necessarily presupposes the order of Nature ;
(2) How it is yet distinct from the order of Nature and constitutes a world apart ;
(3) In what the dynamism of Freedom consists and what is the essential law of its movement.

I

2. The order of Freedom necessarily presupposes the order of Nature ; of Nature in its metaphysical meaning and above all as the nature of a being endowed with intellect and will. This doctrine may be verified first of all in relation to Free Will itself. And ought not we to begin our study with an inquiry into the meaning of Free Will ? All the varied senses of the word Freedom which have importance for mankind presuppose this primordial freedom, this fact that our Will in its inner fortress is free not only from all external constraint but also from any kind of inherent necessity that would determine it *ad unum*.

In the teaching of St. Thomas freedom of choice is not an irrational element thrust on the philosopher by the moral consciousness ; it is a thing proper to a certain *nature*, in short, to the rational or intellectual nature. " The whole root of freedom lie in reason."[1] To be free is of the essence of every intellectual being.

Not only therefore do we experience within us the fact of freedom, through our awareness that the act which emanates from our deliberate will is so dependent on us as to be ours to the very essence of its being and even to the reason which elicits it ; but it is also possible (for the Thomist) to show that an intellectual being is *of necessity* endowed with freedom.

Every appetite (or, in modern terminology, every faculty that manifests tendency or inclination) is a power by which the subject directs himself towards Being in concrete shape in order either to incorporate it in his own self or to incorporate himself in it. It is this attractive or *directive* function of Being in relation to appetite that gives rise to the notion of ontological Good or Good-in-general and that likewise explains why every appetite is dependent upon knowledge. By the sensitive appetite the irrational animal tends (spontaneously and necessarily, as a result of the totality of its actual dispositions) towards the particular and concrete ' good ' that its senses make known to it but without investing this good with the objective character of the Good ; for the senses have no more knowledge of the Good *as such* than of Being or the One *as such*. It is by our will that we direct ourselves towards things that are good as known to us by our intellect, towards things, that is to say, that are known to us in their character as good. The intellect which abstracts and recognizes the objective

---

[1] St. Thomas, *De Veritate*, q. 24, a. 2.

form of Being abstracts and recognizes also the objective form of Goodness—a thing which is beyond the power of purely sensitive faculties. In every nature endowed with intellect there ought therefore to be found a power of loving and desiring essentially distinct from the sensitive appetite and tending to the Good *as such*, to the Good in the universal and transcendental character in which it comprehends each several good. This power we call the rational appetite or will.

The will is thus founded in Nature and is itself a kind of nature. And since it is thus a nature, it has a necessary end or determination : there is something it desires by *virtue of what it is* : this something is the Good *as such*. The will tends *of necessity* to Something of which all it knows is that it satisfies all desire.

What then ? If the will is *necessarily* directed to a good that has no limit, it follows that any good which is not a good without limit cannot bind the will by its necessity. It is because the will has by nature a capacity for the infinite and because it tends by nature and necessarily to an infinite Good which shall fulfil its aspiration that the will is free in face of every particular and partial good, of every good that we can take and measure and that is insufficient to exhaust the infinite capacity of the will to love. If then we decide to will such and such a good, we have none the less the power not to will it. In other words, our will has power to endow the thing it wills with the attraction that thing exercises.

The schoolmen called this freedom of the will ' indifference,' but they were careful to explain

7

that this notion of ' indifference ' in no way coincides with the indetermination of a thing in potency to be, which is still unformed and awaits determination and has the capacity to become this or that thing, to receive this or that act. The indifference which is proper to the will is of an active and dominant kind and springs from the spiritual fulness of a faculty which being excited to act and to appetite by the Infinite has no necessary bond with finite things.

In fine, if in every will there exists this lofty indifference to finite things the reason is that in every being short of Infinite Being there is inability to constrain the will to choose. The sum of the ' goods ' that exist are not the Good, and the intellect is aware of it since it has the concept of the Good. And so we see that if freedom presupposes the nature of will it also presupposes, on a deeper level so to say, the nature of intellect.

St. Thomas does not conceive Free Will as a sort of divinity of the noumenal order that lives within us and that nothing can affect. He knows that our free will is immersed in a world of affectivity, of instinct, of passion, of sensitive and spiritual desire. Our will is solicited on every side ; it is weak ; it loves and desires all sorts of ' goods ' in its own despite. But when our intellect intervenes to deliberate our action it awakens the infinite capacity for love of which we have been speaking : to will and to love this or that good to the point at which it determines my act, the act of my human personality, this is proper to the free action of my will, for it depends on a practical judgment of my intellect which my will alone is able to control.

My intellect may indeed adjudge in a speculative way that such an action should be done ; but that does not make me do it. This needs a practical decision, a practical judgment of the intellect. And when the mind deliberates it sees that every limited good in so far as it is limited is in one view good, and in another view not good ; that it is at once acceptable and yet not acceptable : to me who aspire by nature to the Infinite Good. Out of the depths of the will itself must come the efficacy that the particular ' good ' which solicits it needs in order that it may be adjudged unconditionally good for me.

In this connexion the schoolmen taught that at the end of our deliberation, in the instant operation which constitutes the act of the free will, the intellect and the will determine one another in different ways, in accordance with the axiom of Aristotle : *causae ad invicem sunt causae.* The diverse causes that co-operate in one act are causes one to another along their different lines of operation. The act of free will thus appears as the common offspring of reason and of will enveloping one another in a vital union ; the practical judgment of reason the effective declaration of which specifies and determines the act of free will derives its actual efficacy from the will itself which transfers (so to say) to the particular and limited good under contemplation the excess of motive power that the will derives from its own determination by the infinite good. The subject thus becomes voluntarily adjusted to this particular good which by the same token comes to be for him unconditionally good and desirable. In conferring

9

its love on things the will endows those things with attraction for it ; in other words, by the efficient action of love, these things come to be objects capable of being the term of an unconditional judgment of the practical reason and are thus competent efficaciously to determine the will itself in the order of formal causality. To be free is to be master of one's judgment, *liberi arbitrii*. The will is able to control the judgment which determines its act and by virtue of this control it has complete mastery of its action.

In this way the philosophy of St. Thomas demonstrates how freedom is an inalienable property of every intellectual or spiritual nature and how it presupposes such a nature, the nature of intellect and the nature of will.

3. This metaphysical primacy of nature over freedom is found again at the summit of Being, in the uncreated world of the Divine perfections.

Some modern philosophers in the tradition of Descartes have thought to see in Freedom that which (so far as our concepts are able to reach it) is the characteristic stuff of the Divine essence. Their thought is of a God existing freely because He wills it so ; of a God who if He willed could annihilate Himself. This opinion would have seemed absurd to the schoolmen, for whom the existence of God is an absolute necessity, Existence being of His very Essence. For the schoolmen God is not at liberty to cease to be or to cease to contemplate His own Being, or to cease to love His own Being, or to cease to live and to enjoy Beatitude. Such is the Divine *Nature*, subject to no necessity or constraint : but in itself and of itself infinitely Necessary.

In knowing Himself God sees in His Essence all the ways in which It may be imitated or participated. The theologians call the ' science of simple intelligence' the knowledge of *possible* created things as pure objects of the Divine Mind prior to their existence in their proper order of nature. In loving Himself God is free to love as He pleases this or that creature which He *may* call into existence : such is the Divine *Freedom*, that belongs to the very Nature of Uncreated Mind.

And here we meet a real difficulty : how can God love or not love, seeing that He is Pure Act and that in Him there is no potentiality ? Does the statement that God is free mean that there is in Him some element of contingency ? By no means, says St. Thomas, there is nothing contingent in the Divine Being. All the contingency is on the side of created things. The answer goes very deep : we shall endeavour to explain it briefly.[1]

It is through the same act of love by which He loves Himself that God loves also that which is not Himself. But He cannot not be the *object* of His love since His love is identical with Himself. Created things being of themselves wholly incapable of exhausting such an infinite Love, the Divine Love possesses an infinite fulness of freedom either to bring them or to abstain from bringing them within the range of its omnipotent causal action. A creature loved by God is not an object which can

[1] Cf. John of St. Thomas, *Curs. Theol.*, Part I, q. 19, disp. 4, a. 3, 4 and 5 (Vivès, Vol. III).

determine or specify the love of God so as to make it dependent on that creature. It is an effect of the love of God ; it is given its specific existence by the Divine love by which the creature is loved and made an object of love and on which the creature wholly depends. Thus for St. Thomas the Divine Freedom is the necessary act of God loving His own essence and goodness, an act which for this very reason is intrinsically free as regards created things. For in regard to everything that is not God Himself it comprehends at once in its sublime simplicity the whole order of things willed and things not willed ; of things loved and things not loved. That one thing be willed and loved (and so called to existence) and that another thing be not so, means that this act of sovereign power which is entirely independent of both lays hold of one thing and not of the other, and makes it in this or that degree an object—of necessity a non-necessary object—of the uncreated love. If nothing else had been loved by God, nothing else would have existed. And this would involve no change in Him. And yet for the creature there is nothing more real than to be loved by God ; it then partakes in some way of the love that God has for Himself. The love of each particular creature is in God something intrinsic and formal and supremely real since it is His immanent act of subsisting Love and of absolute Freedom in face of every possible being which constitutes this particular creature, this thing and not another, as the object of His love.

According to St. Thomas, then, the existence of the Divine Nature necessarily involves, by virtue of the Eternal wisdom, the possibility of created things and necessarily involves also (antecedently to the existence of created things) an absolute Freedom in God to love these things and (by His love) to bring them into actual existence : a subsisting Freedom which is God Himself and which cannot not be exercised. Whether things are or whether they are not in fact willed or loved and brought into being, whether creatures exist or do not exist, it is always and equally this same Freedom that explains all. Here also at the summit of all Being, the philosophy of St. Thomas reveals to us Freedom with its roots in nature, in the nature, that is, of spiritual being : and in the Being of God inseparable from It—and indeed one with It, for the Divine Freedom in face of created things is identical with the necessary Love wherewith God loves Himself ; and with the very Essence of the Divine Being.

4. But that Freedom presupposes Nature, what does this mean for us ? It means that ethics presupposes metaphysics and speculative philosophy and that the true use of our freedom presupposes the knowledge of Being and of the supreme laws of Being. Metaphysics is a necessary prerequisite of ethics.

This truth is masked sometimes, since man, who carries within him the same realities—soul, freedom, the call of destiny—which metaphysics has to study and to know, and who thus lives the life of metaphysics before his mind has grasped its principles, man, I say, can afford the luxury of denying in theory the metaphysical truths of which in practice he makes considerable use. It is plain, however, that such a situation is not normal and that it is of supreme importance for man to take cognisance of all the things that integrate him ; and of the true dimensions of his being.

The very crises of the economic order urge us strongly to study metaphysics. Competent writers tell us that the most terrible economic crises of modern times with their absurd consequences— here corn and coffee are destroyed by burning, there millions of workmen are out of work—spring from the rationalisation on scientific lines of the technical processes of production or more generally of the material of economic life without any corres- ponding rationalisation of production itself or of the human elements in the economic order. But it is no more possible to rationalise the human elements without knowing what man is than to rationalise the production of a factory without knowing what a factory is. We must know then what man is : which is the office of metaphysics and even of theology. Ethics, which we may consider as the rationalisation of the use of Freedom, presupposes metaphysics as its necessary prerequisite. A system of ethics cannot be constituted unless its author is first able to answer the questions : *What is man ? Why is he made ? What is the end of human life ?*

Man is a metaphysical being, an animal that nourishes its life on transcendental things. There is no ethic among ants any more than among the stars; the road they are to follow is traced out for them in advance. But we men, merely because we know the sense of the word *Being* and of the word *Why*, and because into our poor head the whole heavens (and more than the heavens) can be fitted, we are lost before we take our first step. We must lay out the road we follow ; we must deliberate our end.

There is here, in truth, on the threshold of ethics a fact of nature, the fact of a spiritual nature. So soon as we act in the character of men, that is to say under the direction of reason, we cannot not will a last end for the sake of which all the rest is willed, and in which the infinite good of which we have spoken takes concrete shape. What is the absolute good ? Where shall we find this beatitude ? It is our business to discover it ; we are metaphysicians in spite of ourselves. We are obliged to make a choice of ends : it is the beginning of our moral life.

In the opinion of St. Thomas[1] we first make a decision as to our last end at the time when the life of reason and of personality comes to establish itself in childhood—a thing which may be accomplished in utter silence in the depths of our being but which is in essence a very great event.

Adults are usually inclined to make light of childhood. They forget that their world of reason, civilised and corrupt, depends in awful measure on the intuitive and tempestuous life of childhood ; and that the most important decisions which control their whole future life have most often been taken in the course of their life as children. Freud has insisted on the importance of the instinctive life of

[1] *Summa theol.* i-ii, 89

childhood. St. Thomas teaches us to recognise also the importance of the spiritual life of the child ; of the first dawning of Freedom. Every time a man pulls himself together in order to think out his last end and to decide his destiny, he is in some sense back again at the absolute beginnings that mark the dawn of reason in the child.

We may here call attention to two points in the philosophy of St. Thomas. In the first place, when a man after deliberating on the problem of life decides to follow the love of that which is good-in-itself (of the *bonum honestum*) and to make his future depend on this decision, it is towards God, even though he know it not, that he orients his life. In the second place, such a choice of God as his last end is an act in conformity with the truth of things ; for it is a truth of nature, a fact of the ontological order, that created intelligence can only find beatitude in God, and perfect beatitude in God seen face to face.[1] This is a prime truth that St. Thomas establishes at the beginning of the section of the *Summa* that deals with moral philosophy. And to this prime truth there corresponds a primary duty, a primary moral obligation, which is to choose this end (which is God) for our last end. It is a commandment laid on liberty by truth. And no egoism or hedonism of a transcendental kind intervenes (as Kant supposed) in the choice which

---

[1] That *perfect* beatitude or the vision of the Divine Essence is *possible* to created intelligences (with the aid of a supernatural exaltation) is a truth certified by faith. It needs nothing short of theological faith to assure me that it is possible for me, a man, to be perfectly happy. Cf., J. Maritain : *Les Degrés du Savoir*, p. 562, note 1 ; *Réflexions sur l'Intelligence*, pp. 132-133.

is thus prescribed by the nature of things ; for the choice of such an end which is absolute Goodness is made from a love that puts the Good before all things else and that subordinates self to it.

It is here, as we said just now, that our ethical life commences. It is here, to be exact, that like a world apart the world of Freedom begins to loom before our eyes.

It will assist our understanding of this matter if we consider for a moment the thought of the East and more particularly Hindu thought. One might almost say that the metaphysics of transmigration is the exact contrary of the metaphysics of the final end. A Christian soul which knows the supernatural value of the least movement of the will can accept the truth that the unhappy life of man, with all its insignificance, its blundering, and its wretchedness opens suddenly out upon Eternity. We imagine, however, that a soul naturally religious but non-Christian, like the soul of India, is apt to be discouraged by such an idea and to take refuge in what we may call an infinite extension of time, as if a series of new lives offered to the same soul would somehow avail to attenuate the disproportion between the precariousness of the journey and the importance of its term. But then there is no longer a term ; Time continues always to be Time. The mind finds itself confronted with the horror of an endless series of reincarnations. The idea of Nirvana appears as a way of escape. But Nirvana is a deliverance from Time. It is quite different from, in a sense it is the exact opposite of, the passage to Eternity and the possession of our last End.

We are convinced that as in India there are to be found true and eminent examples of moral virtue, so also there exists a real and profound spiritual life in which (whatever be the way of his metaphysical thinking) man turns to God as to his end. In this place, however, we are concerned not with ways of living but with ways of thinking ; with moral science and philosophy. And so we ask : what consequences ensue in the ethical order from this omission in metaphysics of the last end ? It is sometimes said that India has no science of ethics. We think it is an error to say so. But it does seem true to say that in the thought of India the moral order is not conceived in its specific character as the proper world of Freedom and of human action.

Just because it does not hear or answer the first call that is made to Freedom, and because it does not require of man the choice of a last end, and the ordering of all his life towards this end, the ethics of Hinduism remains enmeshed in the world of Nature and its linked order of events ; human acts are deemed to produce results in much the same way as if they belonged to the physical order, and even asceticism follows the advance of knowledge in an almost automatic way ; the idea of moral obligation is never elucidated, and ethics is never allowed to escape from the shadows of time and of *maya*. Indeed the moral order is doomed to vanish with the shadows when the day of perfect knowledge shall dawn.

I pray the reader to excuse the digression. It may help to make clear to what extent ethics (if it is to maintain its own separate and distinct existence) must presuppose and depend on meta-physics. And ethics thus depends on metaphysics not only for the determination of the last end of man but also for a knowledge of the laws which govern the choice of means and which constitute its proper domain. According to St. Thomas these laws arise immediately from the rational nature of man (for reason supplies the proximate rule of human action) and ultimately from what Christian philosophy calls the Eternal law,[1] that is to say, the ideal order of creation in the mind of the Creator, an order which becomes manifest to our intellect whenever it sees, beyond the existing scheme of reality, the ordinances that are inscribed in the nature of things, and in particular the rule which ordains that the first test of the goodness or badness of a human act is afforded by its object. But the ability thus to seize the essential prescriptions and necessities of things presupposes that our intellect has power not only (like our senses) to ascertain and verify things in an experimental fashion but also to pene-trate into the inner being and structure of essences.

Doubtless for the proper formation of moral science there is required much speculative knowledge beside metaphysics and above all an immense amount of information of an experimental kind. St. Thomas goes the length of saying that the things pertaining to moral science are known especially through experience.[2] It is none the less true that metaphysics supplies the first foundation.

[1] Cf. St. Thomas, *Summa theol.*, i-ii, 71, 6 ; 93, 5, corp. et ad 3.
[2] " Quae pertinent ad scientiam moralem maxime cognoscuntur per experientiam." *In Ethic. Nic.*, lib. I, lect. 2.

Ethics then rests entirely on speculative knowledge. But ethics—and here we reach the second part of our study—is not itself a science of the speculative order : it is a practical science. Metaphysics is necessary, yet it is not sufficient to constitute moral science. Moral philosophy is not a department of metaphysics ; it has a sphere of its own wholly distinct from the order of speculative science.

II

According to St. Thomas the first division of knowledge (of the knowledge of created beings, that is to say) is the division between speculative and practical science, between speculative and practical philosophy.[1] Speculative science has knowledge itself for its intrinsic end : it seeks knowledge for the sake of knowing. Practical science has for its intrinsic end something other than mere knowledge : its knowledge is for action. Such is the first line of cleavage in human science. Now ethics belongs to the practical order. It is a species of knowledge, a true science, but one which has in view a practical object : *acts to be done*. For ethics therefore, the ends for which we act, which here means the ends of human life, play a part corresponding to that which first principles play in speculative science. It is not possible to have a

[1] Theology alone, by reason of the supernatural exaltation of its principles and because it is in some sense a participation or an impression in us of Uncreated Wisdom, transcends this division and keeps its unity.

science of numbers except by reference to the principles of mathematics. Neither is it possible to have a science of ethics except by reference to the ends of human action. " Of things to be done," writes St. Thomas, " we have a perfect understanding only so far as we know their principle of operation."[1]

It follows that although it examines and utilises a great mass of material alike of the speculative and of the experimental order the science of ethics is none the less not a science of simple statement or verification. As science and philosophy it seeks to know what is right to be done, and how it may be done so that it shall be well done. And it is also evident that the science of ethics is a science of Freedom. Though there may be a speculative science of the nature of Free Will there cannot be a speculative science of the use of Free Will. There is a practical science of the use of Free Will : it is the science of ethics.

Here the intellect penetrates into the proper domain of the will. It is scarcely surprising that St. Thomas, who is so purely intellectualist in metaphysics, should show himself more and more voluntarist in the measure in which his study concerns action as such. The typical object of ethical science is something willed (human acts) but it is according to a speculative norm[2] that this science judges human acts and the rules of human action. For this reason, though ethics is a practical science, it is not fully capable of regulating these acts. To enable me to know and judge with perfect and constant rectitude

---

[1] *Summa Theol.*, i, 14, 16, ad cont.
[2] Cf. *Les Degrés du Savoir*, pp. 618-625 and Annexe VII.

the individual acts that I have to do—I, an individual person, in such and such individual circumstances which have never before existed and will never exist again in precisely the same combination—no science, though it be a practical science, and no system of casuistry will ever suffice. For science is properly of universals. I need a means of knowledge and of practical judgment that is more than a science. I need the virtue of prudence : a virtue that resides in the reason but is also of the moral order seeing that it can only judge rightly if the will too is rectified ; for prudence controls the exercise of my freedom immediately, not from a distance. Prudence is integrated with the other moral virtues ; it presupposes that I know what justice and what temperance require not merely by way of theory but in an experimental way by the connatural knowledge that comes of the habitual exercise of these virtues. And in this connexion St. Thomas says that a knowledge of metaphysics (however necessary it may be as a basis for ethical science) is useless as a guarantee of right conduct, and that a knowledge of ethics (for all its necessity in turn) is of very little value for the purpose.[1]

Another spiritual principle is needed, prudence in the intellect ; and, in the sensitive powers, stable dispositions which will prepare and fortify us to make a right use of our freedom.

One sees how in the philosophy of St. Thomas the world of ethics is a world apart, a realm of action distinct from the realm of speculation, a realm of Freedom distinct from the realm of Nature.

[1] *Sent.*, iii, d. 33, q. 2. a. 5, ad I ; d. 35, q. i. a. 2, ad i.

6. If we wish to picture to ourselves the universal order of reality in degrees or grades as St. Thomas saw it, we shall have to put at the base of our diagram the world of sensible things, things subject to time and movement : the world of sensible nature.

Above this world, and forming so to say the superior level of creation comes the world of spiritual things : these also have being and nature ; we use again the word ' nature ' but in a very pure sense which retains only an analogy to its former meaning : for we are concerned now with the intelligible or ontological constitution of things without any admixture of elements of sense or imagination. Leibniz called this world of spiritual nature the Kingdom of Souls. It is outside the order of sensible nature, but not beyond the limits of creative power.

Now on the same level and in the heart of the same universe we may see the beginnings of another world : it is the world of Freedom. It presupposes spiritual natures, as we have said. But it constitutes a world apart, distinct from the world of nature both sensible and spiritual.

Nor must we forget : the Thomist picture of reality does not stop there. At a third level which no figure can circumscribe, there is yet another universe, this one truly supernatural, beyond the limits of creative power : it is the uncreated universe of the Godhead where Nature now Divine and Freedom also Divine coincide (as we have seen) in one Absolute.

In this universe of the Divine Existence the human soul can participate by grace, so that for the

human soul also there is a third stage truly supernatural where *a new nature* (of the divine order)
is given to it and where *the world of Freedom*, that
world apart which began on the level just below,
reaches its perfection in the divine order. But we
do not desire now to speak of this universe of Grace.
We are concerned with the world of Freedom as it
exists on the second stage and exhibits the inseparable property of a certain kind of created nature—
the spiritual nature.

Two other points in the philosophy of St. Thomas
may here be emphasized. In the first place St.
Thomas teaches that at the head of the world of
nature, of every created nature, of sense and spirit,
and at the head also of the world of freedom is God.[1]

In the world of Nature God appears as the last
end and the omnipotent ruler of the universal order ;
and from this point of view we may say He has no
adversary and that there is no resistance to His Will.
Evil and Good, death and life, the failure and the
splendour of created things, what He is pleased to
permit, what He is pleased to call into being, all
is equally caught and invincibly borne along in the
torrent of reality that expresses His sovereign
Wisdom. In the world of Freedom, God appears as
legislator and as end of that special order which
constitutes the moral order, and from this point of
view He has adversaries, for He permits created
spirits to resist His Will, which is ideally manifest
to them as the supreme rule or norm of Freedom.
In this wise the world of Nature and the world of

[1] Cf. *Summa theol.*, i, 103, 5, 7, and 8, and the *Commentary of
Cajetan.*

Freedom have the same head. This truth was overlooked by the Manichean and Gnostic thinkers, for whom the author of Nature was not God, the ruler of the moral order, but a Demiurge or even the principle of evil. They were poor metaphysicians, who discredited the world of Nature in order to exalt the world of Freedom. On the other hand the world of Freedom is so radically autonomous that, although it constitutes a special order in the midst of the universal order and even by virtue of this fact, we must mount to the first principle of the universe if we are to find its proper head. The First Cause of all things thus guarantees the irreducibility of this particular order of moral Good and Evil to the universal order of Being. It is a truth that escaped a great metaphysician like Spinoza, who sought for Freedom not in the world of Freedom (which he omitted from his philosophy) but in the world of Nature. The author of the *Ethics* sacrificed Ethics to Metaphysics.

The second point we wish to emphasize concerns the inviolability of the order of Freedom. St. Thomas elucidates the point when he is handling a very special issue. He asks if the natural vision of pure spirits can penetrate the inner secrets of the heart. And his reply is in the negative. Yet he teaches elsewhere that pure spirits have a natural knowledge of the whole order of corporal and spiritual nature, of all the events which happen *in this world*, which is the work of creative art. And truly it is so ; but the moral act taken precisely as such, in the mystery of the free choice it makes before the face of God, is not an event *in this world ;*

it does not belong to the world of forms and pro-
perties of things, or (shall we say) of simple plastic
and ontological beauty of creation ; it belongs to
the world of Freedom which even in the natural moral
order (prescinding altogether from the supernatural
order of grace) is a world apart, cloistered, sacred,
where the vision of God alone has right or power to
penetrate. For it is the world of relations between
intellectual beings, and in particular between the
Personality of the Uncreated Spirit and the persons
whom He has made in His image.

7. And here we meet the most challenging
problem in speculative theology, the problem of the
relations between the Uncreated Freedom and the
freedom of created beings. We do not propose to
discuss it now. We shall recall only that, according
to St. Thomas, God alone knows the secrets of the
Freedom he has created and He alone can act upon
that Freedom. He alone can pierce into those
secret places of the soul. And why ? Because He
is the cause of all the Being of all that is. Wherever
there is being, He is there as First Cause ; and when
I exercise an act of freedom He alone is there, with
me and in me, since, in brief, this act being free
does not depend on any cause within the order of
creation save only me.

And God is cause in an analogical and eminent
sense. He is not cause in the same sense as any of
the causes of which I have experience. He rules and
transcends both the order of Necessity and the
order of Contingence. When therefore He acts in
me who act, His action is to supply the essential

freedom of my act. It is just so far as I am a free agent and have dominion over my act that His power penetrates my being, causing, in His quality as First Cause, in me who am a second and free cause, the very mode of my action and the perfection that is proper to it as a free act.

But what happens when my act is evil ? Of evil itself or of privation, of the mutilation which deforms my act, God cannot be cause : of this it is I who am first cause.[1] Evil as such is the only thing I am able to do without God, by withdrawing myself, as if by an initiative emanating from my nothingness, from the current of Divine Causality. In the line of evil-doing the creature is first cause. *Without me you can do nothing*. The word is true, in two senses : without God we cannot do anything ; we can without Him " do nothing." The first initiative towards good acts comes always from God, so that here the initiative of created Freedom has its origin in the initiative of God. But by reason of the power to refuse, which is a natural element of all created freedom, the first initiative to evil-doing comes always from the creature ; God has the power but does not will to prevent the creature (when it is so inclined) from interposing its refusal. For the hands of God are tied by the inscrutable designs of His love as were those of the Son of Man upon the Cross.

We can thus form some idea of the drama of history or rather of the drama of the sacred element in history. Despite all the mass of sensible material

---

[1] " Defectus gratiae *causa prima* est ex nobis." St. Thomas. *Summa theol.* i-ii, 112, 3, ad 2.

that conditions it in the order of nature, history is fashioned above all things by crossing and commingling, by chase and conflict, of Uncreated Freedom and created Freedom. It is invented (so to say) at every instant by concordant or discordant initiatives of these two types of Freedom, the one within Time, the other outside Time, able in a single glance from the heights of Eternity (where all the movements of Time are indivisibly present) to know the whole succession of things in Time. And the Divine Freedom is all the more wonderful and glorious for the liberty it gives to created Freedom to undo its work ; for only the Divine Freedom can out of a wealth of destruction draw forth a superabundance of Being. But we, poor mortals, who are part of the tapestry of history, are conscious only of the confused tangle of threads that is knotted on our heart.

If we were now asked what is the end to which, amid so many vicissitudes, created freedom is ordered, we should have to contemplate the third stage or level in the picture to which we have referred, and to recall the doctrine of Grace, which is a participation in the very life of God. We should answer then that the end of created Freedom is to reach a point of supreme perfection in which are realised the three primordial postulations of the creature in the presence of the Divine Persons, that is to say, a state of perfection in which in the creature now made holy, the Holiness of God is made manifest in purest light ; the sovereign rule of His Truth is established in power ; and reconciliation is effected (there being now no longer any interposition either of obstacle or of refusal) between His will called ' consequent,' which takes account of circumstances arising from the action of created wills, and His will called ' antecedent,' which issues from His love alone.

In so far as such an end concerns the community of men, it constitutes the only City which imposes on human personality (now purified by death and risen again) neither constraint nor sacrifice, for the common good of this City will be the good also of personality (*et lucerna ejus erit agnus*). This City descends from heaven, but the movement of history goes out towards it.

In so far as such an end concerns the spiritual progress of the soul, it includes, among the many demands it makes, the obligation of passing freely (through all the misfortunes and the accidents that follow our fragility) from a freedom of choice between good and evil (which marks the imperfection of the creature as such) to a freedom always to choose the good, which is the work of the Divine nature and which presupposes the transformation of the soul by Grace and Love.

And so we reach the third part of this essay, in which we deal briefly with what may be called the dynamism of Freedom.

III

8. At this point it is necessary to make an analysis of the meaning or the divers meanings of the word Freedom. So far we have spoken of Freedom in the sense in which the will is free. But the notion

of Freedom is very much wider than the notion of Free Will. Free Will is indeed the source and spring of the world of Freedom : it is a datum of metaphysics ; we inherit it with our rational nature ; we do not have to achieve it : it appears within us as an initial form of Freedom. But this metaphysical root must grow and develop in the psychological and the moral order. We are called upon to become in action what we are already in the metaphysical order : a Person.[1] It is our duty by our own effort to make ourselves *persons* having dominion over our own acts and being to ourselves a rounded and a whole existence. There we have another kind of Freedom, a freedom to gain which we must pay a great price : Freedom in fulfilment. What shall we call it ? We may say it is the Freedom of autonomy. The ancients marked it by the word αὐτάρκεια meaning that the free man is self-sufficient, and by the expression *causa sui* meaning that the free man governs his own life without suffering constraint from any external cause : expressions which taken in their full significance correspond to the true inwardness of the notion of personality. We maintain then that freedom of choice, freedom in the sense of free will, is not its own proper end. It is directed to the achievement of freedom in the sense of *autonomy ;* and in this quest of autonomy which answers to an essential demand of human personality the dynamism of freedom is to be found.

[1] A person is in the classical definition " an individual substance of rational nature " : *individualis substantia rationalis naturae.* The definition is of fundamental importance in philosophy and in law.

This principle has two several applications of peculiar importance, one in the spiritual, the other in the social order.

9. In the order of the spiritual life, we may at once observe that all the sages, stoics, epicureans, and neo-platonists, yogis, rabbis and sufi, spinozists and nietzscheans, have always wished, whatever the name they use, to achieve the one thing: Freedom. All have maintained that its achievement requires a certain measure of asceticism (interpreted in one or other of many different ways) and that it implies a state of perfection beyond ordinary human reach. To propose to man a merely human end, said Aristotle, is to misunderstand his nature. The saying is profoundly true. But if ever it be dangerous for man to err, it is assuredly most dangerous when his mistake concerns the passage to a superhuman state.

What then is the essence of this Freedom which is also wisdom? A prime error which seems to be the root error of many of our contemporaries lies in the confusion of the two kinds of Freedom that we have distinguished: freedom of choice, and freedom of autonomy. This error makes the highest form of freedom consist in freedom of choice; as if the reason for choosing were not to escape having to choose again! Free choice becomes an end in itself, and man, condemned to recurrent acts of choice without ever being able to bind himself, is launched into a dialectic of freedom which destroys freedom. In order always to be ready to make any fresh choice that the circumstances of the moment may suggest, he refuses to declare for an end which, once chosen, would limit the field of possible choices in the future. In order to enjoy as a supreme good the pure exercise of his freedom he refuses to determine it by reference to a rational ground. His effort of asceticism, being thus frustrated by the paradox of a will that has no last end and of a free will that has no root in reason, tends merely to dissipate in indefiniteness and indecision his personality, his freedom, and his capacity for love. For love is always a bond.

Going straight to the heart of the problem, the theologians of the Thomist tradition observe that freedom (in the sense of the freedom of choice) does not constitute the essence or the formal element of moral action, as so many of the modern followers of Kant[1] seem to imagine. Freedom of choice is the *material* element in moral action, since only free acts are capable of being regulated by moral rules, as the matter wrought by the sculptor or the musician is capable of regulation by rules of art. In either case it is reason which gives form and measure. An act is not of more value in morals because it contains a greater measure of freedom ; on the contrary to act for the mere pleasure of acting, solely to exercise one's sense of freedom,

[1] In the system of Kant freedom of autonomy is not the fruit of moral progress but the property and expression of the intemporal freedom of choice which man enjoys in the intelligible world. The two kinds of freedom are here (1) each falsified in idea, (2) confused. And the formal constituent of morals is sought in this false concept of freedom, although of the two kinds of freedom thus confused neither in reality gives the *essence or the formal element* of moral action (for freedom of choice is the *matter* of morals and freedom of autonomy is the *term* towards which it moves).

is apt to be a sign of moral debility. Freedom of choice is a prerequisite to moral action ; it does not constitute it. It is the vital control of the free act by reason, by human reason and even more by the Eternal Reason ; it is *consonance with reason*, as St. Thomas says, that is the *formal* constituent of moral action.

A second error no less serious proceeds from a more sober philosophy. Those who make this error appreciate that the supreme enfranchisement of man lies not in freedom of choice but in the other kind of freedom that we have called freedom of autonomy. And they appreciate also that this freedom of autonomy, defined as the plenary self-sufficiency of a person who does not depend on any external cause, is a species of freedom that is in truth proper to God. But by reason of an imma-nentist prejudice they think that man is called to endow himself out of his own resources with this sovereign Freedom, whether it be freedom of knowledge and pure intellectuality as in the case of the Sage of Spinoza, or of power and creation as in the case of the Superman of Nietzsche. And thus man is obliged to divinise himself by the use of purely natural means, and is ground in a living contradiction between the God that he must be and the creature that he is.

The solution that St. Thomas proposes to this problem is a solution on Christian principles. True, man is called to be divine ; by a participation of grace, he takes on the nature of a God transcend-ent, personal, free. When after the dissolution of his body he reaches his last end he is *God by participation* since he has a vision of the Divine Essence. And even during his earthly life he can, even then, become God by participation through his union of love with God. Thus, it is in sanctity that the perfect freedom of autonomy is found. For sanctity embraces the Freedom (of which we have already spoken) of always choosing the Good, and for this reason, since it thus becomes ignorant of evil, one might also call such freedom the Freedom of Innocence. But it is something more. It is of its own nature a fruit or outcome, and an end ; for it is another name for the perfection of the spirit, and a beginning at any rate of adhesion to the last end.

This adhesion has two aspects : in so far as it relates to the life of intellect, it is wisdom and the full possession of spiritual life, freedom of exultation one might say, for the achievement of the deepest and purest desire of the intellect means life and freedom in repose. In much the same way St. Thomas gives the name *vacatio* to the contemplation of things divine.

In so far as this adhesion relates to the life of the will, it is the plenitude of perfect love and freedom of autonomy. Of these two aspects, the first will appear in its perfect form only in the vision of God, the second has priority in our present life : they are nevertheless inseparable.

It is in order to reach this freedom of autonomy, this terminus of freedom, that man is given freedom of choice. And freedom of autonomy is so little bound up with freedom of choice that in the supreme act of beatitude the latter finds no room for exercise. St. Thomas teaches that the souls of the beatified

34

who contemplate the Divine Essence, being fixed eternally in that vision, are likewise fixed in beatific love, their will adhering to God with all the strength and purpose of a nature made for the infinite Good. How can one make a fresh act of choice when one is at last in possession of that which one has chosen in preference to all ? The power to exercise a free choice will survive in all things else ; it will not survive before subsisting Good seen face to face. And yet nowhere more fully than in the beatitude of love is there freedom of autonomy, for it is in accordance with the very law of its being that the will cannot then not love. There is no act that is more voluntary[1] and yet it no longer exhibits the lofty indifference that is proper to freedom of choice. We find here a perfectly logical return to that primacy of Nature over freedom of choice which was discussed in the first part of this essay. When freedom of choice has led a spiritual nature, endowed in intellect and in will with a capacity for the infinite, to the term for which it is made, its office is accomplished. It always remains of course, for it is the privilege of a spiritual nature, and it continues to manifest the lofty independence of this nature in face of all that is means or intermediate end : but not in the face of that which is the End. At this terminus, however, it is still Freedom but Freedom in another manifestation that comes into play, since this nature being spiritual has its true fulfilment only in spontaneity

[1] On all this discussion and for the capital distinction between *voluntary* and *free* acts, see John of St. Thomas, *Curs. Theol.*, in i-ii, q. 21, disp. 8, a. i. (Vivès, vol. V). [See also Q. 6. disp. 3. Vol. V, pp. 358 seqq. TR.]

that is absolute. And this freedom of exultation and of autonomy is truly, to take a word that is often used but imperfectly understood by modern philosophers, the " perfect spontaneity of a spiritual nature."

Besides, it is not of themselves or by themselves, it is by union with One who is Other and who is Source of all Being and of all Goodness, that created spirits are able to reach such a perfection of spontaneous life. It cannot be otherwise once the matter is viewed in the perspectives of a philosophy of Being and of a metaphysic of Divine Transcendence. Finite and wretched in self, man cannot pass to a super-natural condition save by adhesion of intellect and will to a superior being. God being the perfection of personal existence and man being also, though precariously, a person, the mystery of the achievement of freedom is contained in the relation of these two persons.

And yet it is no technical philosopher, it is St. Paul who reveals to us something of this mystery. Theology teaches that those who are moved by the spirit of God being truly the sons of God are truly and fully free ; and that (as St. John of the Cross says) they enter into the very interior life of the Divine persons, loving God as He loves us and as He loves Himself ; and giving God to God Himself : this is the limit of progress of the soul in which (until the vision that its union with a corruptible body precludes) time is conjoined to eternity. The saint denudes himself of his dominion over his own self in order to give it to God ; and that is possible since God is more intimately in us than we are ourselves ; to lose our soul for Him is thus not to

36

lose it but to find it. It is with the liberty of God Himself that the man of perfect soul is free. He is independent of every external constraint because he is dependent only on the Divine causality which is in no sense stranger to him. He is self-sufficing because he has lost his own self and lives only by the life of the Divine Saviour who lives in him. Far more truly than the sage of pagan thought he is all things to himself since he is now one only in Love and Spirit with the Absolute : " two natures in one Spirit and one Love."[1]

This work is in truth the achievement of Love. Let us glance again at a page of the *Summa contra Gentiles* that we have cited elsewhere ; it gives us the key to the problem of freedom, I mean the Freedom of Autonomy.

" We must observe, however," writes St. Thomas, " that the sons of God are led by the Holy Ghost, not as though they were slaves, but as being free. For, since to be free is to be cause of one's own actions, we are said to do freely what we do of ourselves. Now this is what we do willingly : and what we do unwillingly, we do, not freely but under compulsion. This compulsion may be absolute, when the cause is wholly extraneous, and the patient contributes nothing to the action, for instance, when a man is compelled to move by force. Or it may be partly voluntary, as when a man is willing to do or suffer that which is less opposed to his will, in order to avoid that which is more opposed to it. Now, the Holy Ghost inclines us to act in such a

---

[1] St. John of the Cross : *Spiritual Canticle*, str. 27 (22) Silv., III, p. 132 (320).

way as to make us act willingly, inasmuch as He causes us to be lovers of God. Hence the sons of God are led by the Holy Ghost to act freely and for love, not slavishly and for fear : wherefore the Apostle says (Rom. viii. 15) : *You have not received the Spirit of bondage in fear ; but you have received the spirit of adoption of sons.*

" Now the will is directed to that which is truly good : so that when, either through passion or through an evil habit or disposition, a man turns away from what is truly good, he acts slavishly, in so far as he is led by something extraneous, if we consider the natural direction of the will ; but if we consider the act of the will, as inclined towards a seeming good, he acts freely when he follows the passion or evil habit, but he acts slavishly if, while his will remains the same, he refrain from what he desires through fear of the law which forbids the fulfilment of his desire.

" Accordingly, when the Holy Ghost by love inclines the will to the true good to which it is naturally directed, He removes both the servitude whereby a man, the slave of passion and sin, acts against the order of the will, and the servitude whereby a man acts against the inclination of his will, and in obedience to the law, as the slave and not the friend of the law. Wherefore the Apostle says (2 Cor. iii. 17) : *Where the Spirit of the Lord is, there is liberty,* and (Gal. v. 18) : *If you are led by the Spirit, you are not under the law.*"[1]

---

[1] *Summa contra Gentiles,* iv, 22. Cf. *Summa theol.,* i-ii, 93, 6 : " Per caritatem quam Spiritus sanctus cordibus eorum infundit, *voluntarie* id quod legis est implent."

St. Thomas solves in the same way as St. Paul the fundamental problem of law and liberty. The office of the moral law is that of a pedagogue, to protect and to educate us in the use of freedom. At the end of this period of instruction we are enfranchised from every servitude, even from the servitude of law, since Love has made us one in spirit with the Wisdom that is the source of Law. The perfect soul serves neither law nor fear. This is why expressions like αὐτάρκης and *causa sui*, that pagan philosophy had raised up on the horizon of thought like ideal forms *awaiting* realisation, of which, in fact, it found only misleading instances (for the highest wisdom of the ancients came finally to doubt even the possibility of wisdom), this, I say, is why these expressions in some sort prophetic find their true and real sense only in the saint.

10. We shall meet an analogous problem in the ordering of social life. As a result, it would seem, of the ferment of Christian ideas in Western thought the idea of Freedom dominates the majority of the great political philosophies of modern times. But in what way? And what notion of freedom do these philosophies possess? It is here that controversy begins.

To simplify the matter one may distinguish from the point of view of social life, three philosophies of freedom.

One may build social life on Freedom taken in the sense of *freedom of choice* and as an end in itself—a conception that one may call liberal or individualist, which has rather faded nowadays but which in its

French costume was the ruling fashion in the nineteenth century.

In this conception culture and society have for their essential office the preservation of something given : the free will of Man ; in such a way that all possible acts of free choice may be available and that men may appear like so many little gods, with no other restriction on their freedom save that they are not to hinder a similar freedom on the part of their neighbour. Truth to tell, this political philosophy suffers from an unconscious form of hypocrisy, for it ignores for the benefit of man in the abstract all the heavy and severe burdens that lie on man in real life, the fact being that a limited number are enabled to enjoy this kind of Freedom only by oppression of the remainder of their fellows. The essential values of social justice and the common good are forgotten. And the tragedy inevitable to Freedom taken as an end in itself is unfolded : the absolute right of each part to realise *its* choice tends naturally to dissolve the whole in anarchy and to make impossible any *realisation* of freedom or any achievement of autonomy, within the order and through the instrumentality of social life. In fact to avoid embarrassments of the most serious kind, compensating mechanisms of the empirical order are brought into play which tend in their turn to reduce to a legal fiction the ideal of individual freedom that had been presented as an absolute principle ; so that in the end the dream of such a culture would seem to be the construction of a positive system of social machinery (as eternal and as complicated as the Aristotelian system of the spheres) set in motion not by pure Wisdom[1] but by the general Will; and having within it a multitude of bourgeois *Ends-in-Themselves* with unlimited freedom to own and to trade and to enjoy the pleasures of life.

A second political philosophy rightly thinks that social life should be based not on freedom of choice, which we have called Initial Freedom, but on terminal Freedom, the Freedom of Autonomy. But this philosophy conceives Freedom of Autonomy as a type of transitive action, expressing itself in production and control; in material accomplishment, in the realisation of power. It is at the hands of the political community itself or of the State that this philosophy seeks the fulfilment of freedom in the field of history, for it sees in the State the highest manifestation of forces pregnant with futurity. One may call this conception of freedom imperialist or dictatorial. It makes its way steadily in the world in German and Russian dress.[2]

In this case freedom of the individual, freedom of choice, and freedom of autonomy give way before

[1] In the French text, *Pensée de la Pensée,* which is the usual French rendering of an almost untranslatable text of Aristotle. Tr.

[2] In Hegel especially this *dynamic* conception of Freedom finds its concrete expression in the Freedom and Power and Achievement that are incarnate in the State, and that come into being with the State and through its action. Since the time of Hegel this conception seems to have dominated the thought of German philosophers and historians; whilst the thought of France in the nineteenth century continued to be controlled by Jean Jacques Rousseau and by the conception of freedom of an abstract and *static* kind, given to the individual with his very being and which it behoves him to preserve as his essential dignity. It has often been observed that the same principle which made freedom the basis of law and a privilege truly divine has given rise to two currents of thought in violent opposition.

the grandeur of the common task. And a different dialectic comes into play : to assure the success of the communal undertaking there is expended a store of energy and of virtue which presupposes the freedom of the individual and which the very principle of this new culture is designed to exhaust. The Collective God of a million arms tends also of his own nature to his own destruction.

Here also no doubt human nature will make spontaneous adjustments and supply men with substitutes for the spiritual life and with personal reasons for offering themselves as sacrifices to social utility, so that in the long run the dream of such a culture would seem to be the production of a Leviathan dominating the whole earth, to the Freedom of which a multitude of happy slaves will gladly sacrifice their souls.

To what political philosophy in its turn does the conception of freedom that we have expounded lead ? According to this philosophy civil society is essentially ordered not to the freedom of choice of each citizen but to a common good of the temporal order which provides the true earthly life of man and which is not only material but also moral in its scope. And this common good is intrinsically subordinated to the eternal good of individual citizens and to the achievement of their freedom of autonomy.

In other words the common good in the temporal order is an intermediate (not a final) end. It has a distinctive character of its own which marks it off from the last end and the eternal interests of human personality ; but part of its very essence is its subordination to that end and to those interests from which it takes its directing norms or standards. It has its own integrity and its proper good but only on the strict condition that it acknowledges this subordination, and does not exalt itself to the level of an absolute good. The fixed and absolute centre from which it takes its bearing is not within the State but outside it. It is essential therefore that the State shall suffer the attraction of and take its direction from a superior order of life (which it promotes in greater or lesser measure in the divers types of political society) and that it shall take the impress and foster the beginnings of something that transcends its own nature. It follows that political society—if it has not the office (which belongs to a superior jurisdiction) of guiding human beings to their spiritual perfection and to their full freedom of autonomy, in other words to Eternal Life—is none the less essentially directed, even through the temporal end that gives the State its character, to the establishment of social conditions which will secure for the mass of men such a standard of material, intellectual, and moral life as will conduce to the well-being of the whole community ; so that every citizen may find in it a positive help in the progressive achievement of his freedom of autonomy.

If this freedom of autonomy had its highest expression in the heroism of arms, as in military civilisations, or in nobility of mind as in the aristo-cratic civilisation of Athens or the hieratic civilisation of India, it would be nonsense to maintain this conclusion as to the end of the social community : the well-being of the latter would be established and fulfilled in a minority of the citizens by the degradation of the majority—as slaves or pariahs—to a less than human status.

We speak of freedom of autonomy in its pure and simple meaning and not in a relative sense only. This freedom of autonomy finds its highest type in the Saint. And by a paradox as wonderful as it is strange, this type of perfection which is one of supernatural exaltation makes an appeal to men of every condition, for it is achieved through the operation of a good will in the secret heart of man. A civilisation, then, the common good of which is referred to a type so transcendent, should necessarily aim at securing for the mass of its citizens conditions that are worthy of man and that will put each citizen thus equipped for the life of reason and of virtue in the way of advancing towards perfect freedom and of achieving his eternal destiny.

Even in its lowliest origins the life of reason and of virtue is a message and a promise, a beginning of advance. And though the development of the moral and rational life of man may not define the immediate and proper end of the political community, it is none the less the most important of the values by reference to which (in the measure in which the right ordering of the community as such permits its achievement) this end is constituted. The political community, like the family group, thus promotes in the individual citizen the beginnings of a work that the individual brings to its term as member of a community of a superior order. In the state of pure nature this higher community would have been, in the language of Leibniz, a metaphysical

City of God and the Spirits ; in actual fact it is the Church, whose supernatural life is communicated under visible forms or in a manner entirely invisible to all men of good will.

Political philosophy, being thus directed not towards pure and simple freedom of choice, nor towards the realisation of Freedom of power and dominion over the external order of nature and history, but towards the realisation and progress of the spiritual freedom of individual persons, will make of justice and friendship the true foundations of social life. It will put in the foreground, as the principal object of social communication and exchange, the goods of the moral order that spring from the immanent activity proper to spiritual natures whose interior principle belongs to a realm more sacred than the state. To those things of truly human worth it orders all the material goods and all the technical progress and all the expansion of power which also constitute an essential part of the common good of the State. This presupposes an established rule of reason, a habit of restraint and of temperance, a certain abstinence in the use of material things ; and it presupposes also the social application of the rules of justice and of charity to the acts which express the freedom of choice of individual citizens, such freedom of choice being always respected as a privilege of human personality, but never idolised. A social culture based on these principles would combine in a higher unity the conflicting elements to which the one-sided conceptions we have already criticised respectively attach an exclusive value. For it is neither free

45

will nor power but wisdom and goodness, the authentic freedom of autonomy that makes the *civis praeclarus*, which contribute to social life its element of greatest value. By virtue of the *dynamism of freedom* we have described it would extend from the state of *initial freedom* or freedom of choice (through which the constitution of the political community, having its origin, preparation and plan in nature, reaches its fulfilment as a work of reason and of virtue) *to the terminal or spiritual freedom* of its citizens, the business of the community being to provide conditions and means that will take account of the common good of the temporal order, and to promote certain beginnings and aspirations the complete achievement of which transcends the order that is proper to social life and the terrestrial City.

11. Such a political philosophy which is neither individualist nor imperialist may be called at one and the same time *communal* and *personal*. It goes without saying that the word ' communal ' has not here the very special sense given to it by the disciples of Le Play, the representatives of what is called the school of ' social science ' who set in contrast ' communal ' and ' particularist ' organisations. It means that civil society is ordered to a common good which is specifically other than the simple arithmetical sum of the particular goods of the citizens taken singly and nobler (taking them both on the same plane) than the individual good. As for the expression ' personal ' it has its full significance only by reference to the Thomist distinc-

tion between the formal aspect of individual and the
formal aspect of person. " The Christian City," we
wrote in the *Three Reformers*, " is as fundamentally
anti-individualist as it is fundamentally *personal*."[1]
More recently the term has been taken by new
schools of thought as the distinctive mark of a new
conception of the world. Used systematically, it
may perhaps run some risk of metaphysical hyper-
trophy. In any event it will be worth while here
to give a more exact statement of its meaning.

The notion of person is an *analogous* notion
which is realised in different degrees and on essentially different planes of ontological being. The
human being is a person, that is to say a universe
or whole of a spiritual nature, endowed with freedom
of choice and intended to enjoy freedom of autonomy.
He is no more a *pure person* that he is *pure intellect.*
On the contrary, just as he is at the lowest level of
intellectual beings, so is he also at the lowest level
of personality. To forget this would be to confuse
the personality of man with the personality of
Angels or again of the Divine Persons in Whom alone
(because the Divine Person is subsistent Being and
subsistent Freedom of Autonomy) is realised in
purest form—in Pure Act—the perfection denoted
by the word Personality, which is, as St. Thomas
says, the highest perfection that exists in the whole
realm of Nature.[2]

It is in man who is animal and also spirit that the
characteristic law of individuation enters most

[1] *Trois Réformateurs*, 1925, p. 32. English translation (Sheed
& Ward), p. 23.
[2] " Persona significat id quod est perfectissimum in tota
natura." *Summa theol.*, i, 29, 3.

deeply into composition with that of personality and tends to thwart it. For the metaphysical root of personality is the subsistence of Spirit and, in all corporal beings, the root of individuality lies in Matter. This is the reason why *personality* in the case of man is precarious and always in peril and must be achieved by a kind of progress.

"The whole theory of 'individuation'" (we wrote elsewhere[1]) "shows that for St. Thomas the individual as such is a *part*.[2] On the other hand, for St. Thomas, the idea of personality as such bespeaks the independence of a *whole*. It alone, in common with the notion of object of knowledge, denotes a term which though making one with something else in no way implies the rôle of *a part*. This is the reason why God who cannot " enter into composition " with anything at all nor be part of a whole cannot be united by Himself to a creature except as an object of knowledge in the beatific vision (*in ratione puri termini objectivi*) or as a Person in the Incarnation (*in ratione puri termini personalis*). In the Holy Trinity the idea of Personality reaches the plenitude of Pure Act. We have there a society divinely perfect where three Persons equal and consubstantial have for common good their own Nature and where each is as much as the three together, in other words, where the notion of individuation and part has entirely disappeared."

"In rebus creatis unus est pars duorum, et duo

---

[1] *Three Reformers*, pp. 195-6.
[2] Even in the angel, where the principle of individuation is not the matter but the specific essence, it is because the essence— which is really distinct from existence and in potency to it—is the ground of multiplicity that it is also the ground of individuation.

trium, ut unus homo duorum, et duo trium," sed " sic non est in Deo, quia tantus est Pater quanta tota Trinitas."[1]

Thus the Person as such aspires naturally to the social life ; it is a whole which seeks to be united to other wholes in spiritual exchanges of intellect and of will.[2] There can be a society of pure persons ; but a society of pure persons is possible only in God where in the members of the society is absent every character of part and where the good of all is in strict and simple truth the good of each Person, for it is the Essence of each.

Everywhere else the persons who are members of the Society are also parts of it ; that is to say, the society is not a society of pure persons but a society of persons who are also individual beings, whether individuals of a *kind* like men, or *individual species* like angels. For a person is part of a society, not pursuant to the formal aspect or characteristic law of *personality* (since to speak of a person is to speak of a whole, not a part) but pursuant to the formal aspect or characteristic law of *individuation*. By reason not of the nature of society and of persons, but of the essential imperfection of the one and the other in the created order and especially in the human order, the common good of a society of created beings will necessarily be different from the proper good of each person within the society, and each person will be a member only by virtue of his being a part.[3]

---

[1] *Summa theol.*, i, 30, 1, ad 4.
[2] M. l'Abbé Daniel Lallement has developed this truth in his lessons of sociology which we trust may soon be published.
[3] " Quaelibet persona singularis comparatur ad totam communitatem, sicut pars ad totum." St. Thomas, *Summa theol.*, ii-ii, 64, 2.

It follows that each person is part or member of political society but not to the whole extent of his being and his existence[1]; he is member or part by virtue of the mark of individuation that he bears. " It is because he is first an individual of a species that man, having need of the help of his fellows to perfect his specific activity, is consequently a citizen of the City, a member of the social body."[2] Being a member of society so that he may satisfy the demands of his personal life, he is member only as part because of his character as *individual*. Hence it appears that the common good of the temporal order is essentially subordinated, in accordance with the theory already propounded, to the extra-temporal good of the human being taken in his quality of *Person*, that is to say, as a whole endowed with a spiritual life and called to a destiny outside Time; and that nevertheless the temporal good of the human being taken in his quality of *individual* or part of the Temporal order is subordinated to the well-being of this whole order, which as such is superior. It is thus in the nature of things that man should surrender his temporal goods and if necessary even his life for the welfare of the community; and that social life should impose on him as an individual, as part of the whole, many restraints and sacrifices. And again, by reason not of the essential character of social life but of certain accidental imperfections that very often occur in it, the things of highest value in his life as a person are in danger of being impaired

---

[1] " Homo non ordinatur ad communitatem politicam secundum se totum et secundum omnia sua." *Ibid.*, i-ii, 21, 4 ad 3.
[2] *Trois Réformateurs*, p. 31 ; English Edition, p. 22.

and degraded by this same social life which is apt
to keep the spiritual development of its citizens at
its own level and thus to hinder instead of helping
it ; *quoties inter homines fui, minor homo redii* . . .

This difference of level between the plane on
which man lives his *personal* life and the plane he
occupies as *part* of a social body illustrates the
metaphysical differences of level which lie at the
centre of all created being and especially of our
human being and which in a word have their
first source and origin in the elements of potency
and act that go to constitute created being. It
explains why personality seeks social life and tends
always to travel beyond it until it enters at last into
a society of pure persons, that is, into the Society
of the Divine Persons which overwhelms it with the
gift of infinitely more than that to which it could of
its own nature properly aspire. From the family
group (which is more fundamental than the State
since it touches the generic differences between
human beings) man passes to civil society (which
affects specific differences between them) and in the
midst of civil society he feels the need of clubs and
fellowships that will interest his intellectual and
moral life. These he enters of his own free choice
and they assist the soul in its efforts to ascend to
a higher level. In the end these also fail to satisfy
and they cramp the soul which is obliged to pass
beyond them. Above the level of civil society man
crosses the threshold of supernatural reality and
enters a society which is the mystical body of an
incarnate God, and whose office is to lead him to his
spiritual perfection and to full liberty of autonomy

and eternal welfare. The Church is at once Desert and City.[1] Within her precincts She nourishes human personality on a divine food and leads it away from the crowds at the circumference, where the soul finds content in life *inter homines*, towards the deeper solitude at the centre where it finds its chief content in life inter *divinas personas*. At last, in the vision in which the intellect apprehends the Divine Essence, man is more than ever lost in the life of the Church, but the common good of the Church is now unveiled and the human being exalted by supernatural power to share, as a pure personality, in the Uncreated Society of the Divine Persons enters into the Kingdom of God and the Light of Glory. Strive not, ye men, to socialise the life of the spirit. It tends of its own nature to live in society and finds its fulfilment only there.

These reflexions, it will be noticed, give its exact significance to the text of Aristotle so often cited by St. Thomas : the good of the City is more noble, *more divine* than that of the individual. In this, as in many other places, Aristotle has stated a *pure principle* the full significance of which could only be revealed to eyes more fully equipped than those of ancient wisdom. This principle must be taken in its strict and formal meaning : in the scale of values which assesses each person as *part* in relation to the social whole. It follows clearly that the good of the community (I mean the real and authentic common good which involves subordination to the supra-temporal interests of human personality) is higher than the good of the individual citizen

[1] Cf. H. Clérissac, *Le Mystère de l'Eglise*, chap. VI.

in the scale of terrestrial values which rate the citizen as part of the community. But these values do not compare with the dignity and the destiny of the human soul. By virtue of the law of transition to which we have already called attention, human personality emerges again on a level above that on which man the citizen counts only for *a part ;* and on this new level the proper good of personality as such gives man a title to precedence over the City or the State. And yet on this new level the human being finds itself part of a new society whose good in turn is a higher good ; and above it again the soul will emerge unless indeed the last society be the Church itself which has the same Good as the soul. In the Church, though the soul may no more emerge above the community, it remains true that in different ways the rational being is for the community and that the community is for it. For if we think of this Jerusalem as sharing the very life of God which is communicated to it, and every stone as a human member of the City, each stone is for the City ; and, if we think of each stone, that is each member, as sharing the very life of God which is communicated to it, and this Jerusalem as the community which unites them, the City is for each stone. " Mine are the heavens and mine is the earth ; mine are all men ; the just are mine and mine the sinners ; the angels are mine, and the Mother of God, and all things are mine. And even God is mine and for me. What then do you ask and what do you seek, my soul ? Thine is all this and all is for thee."[1]

[1] St. John of the Cross, *Avisos y Sentencias* (Andujar MS.).

Being thus admitted by way of vision into a society that is truly divine, the rational soul and the Church emerge *in patria* above every form of social life, and yet to the extent that they are creatures before the transcendence of the All-in-all, they are there as parts, of which not indeed the proper good (which is identical with the good of the Divine Whole) but their way of possession of It is short of the Being of it and is essentially ordered to it : It is truly *more Divine* for It is the Being of God.

12. In the foregoing we have attempted to define the sense in which a political philosophy based on the right foundations may be called at one and the same time *Communal* and *Personal.* Many other questions ensue with particular reference to the way in which such a conception of the State may be realised in the historical order. For it is evident that it has a wide adaptability and is capable of realisation in different ways, all of them indeed more or less imperfect by reason of original sin which always afflicts mankind.

Is it necessary to insist on the diversity of historical conditions that mark off the Middle Ages from these modern times ? The effort of the Middle Ages, which worked amid the ruins of the pagan world and on a mass of barbarian peoples who were beginning to be civilised, was to raise up to heaven a Terrestrial City that should be the Throne of the King of Glory. To build it they had to make the best of the poor temporal means at their disposal, *quantum potes tantum aude,* and to make use of human material which there was scarcely time to prepare or purify ; but which pure wisdom, in some measure unaware of its own power and intent on external things, was able to mould and dignify. In our own time those who are at work in the heart of a civilisation that was once Christian and that is now in dissolution and declining again towards barbarism have to prepare for a new world less pretentious dwellings that shall afford a shelter to men and where God whom Love always inclines to our weakness may also come and find a shelter for His goodness and His humanity.[1] If such a work is essentially divine, it demands of the creature none the less a very full consciousness of the human factors that are set in motion and a corresponding purification of the means to be used, and a deliberate effort to bring rich temporal means[2] to humble uses and to subject them to the rule of wisdom.

In other essays we have had something to say of this contrast between the medieval and the modern world. Here we desire very briefly to point out that if a *communal* and *personal* society should emerge in modern history, in conditions very different from and even the inverse of medieval conditions, it is likely none the less to reproduce in an analogous fashion certain characteristics of medieval civilisation. We think, for example, that though greatly differing in style it also will be a society of *corporative*, *authoritative*, and *pluralist* type.

---

[1] " Benignitas et humanitas ($\phi\iota\lambda\alpha\nu\theta\rho\omega\pi\iota\alpha$) Salvatoris nostri Dei." St. Paul, Titus, iii. 4.
[2] See p. 133, *infra*.

The corporative and gild[1] organisation as a State form is so strictly in line with the needs of our time that under different names and in the service of different ideals it has already come into being in Soviet Russia and in Fascist Italy. In the City of our imagination that we conjure up in order hypothetically to illustrate our principles—a City which is conceivable only after the dissolution of capitalist society—the economic and political order[2] of civil

[1] Current terminology on this point is very confused. Everyone seems to attach his own meaning to these words " corporative " and " gild " ; and not unnaturally, since the necessities resulting from our economic technique which direct civilisation towards this type of organisation prescribe only *generic* conditions and do not fix a social system. It is the *spirit* which animates such a system, in a word it is moral and human, not merely technical elements, that determine its specific type.

It is not surprising that the word " corporative " is interpreted by some in a sense favourable to state capitalism of a Fascist type, and that the word " gild " is interpreted by others in the sense of a class struggle on the Marxist plan.

These same words are none the less used in Papal documents in an entirely different sense and in a much more general signification.

Our use of them is in the sense that they bear in Christian social philosophy, a sense that is to say which is neither Fascist nor Marxist but *communal* and *personal*.

[2] To our way of thinking the political order must not be confounded with the economic order of society. These two orders are combined in an organic union ; yet one of them, the political order, having a more *formal* and less *material* character, is superior to the other. In our opinion the current tendency to subordinate or reduce or assimilate the political to the economic order is an error arising from a materialist philosophy. However closely united it may be to the economic order of society, the political order of that society ought normally to be supreme. One may consider it as an organic unity in which not only the interests and points of view of bodies of the economic order but also the special interests and the political thought of other bodies, whether domestic, cultural, or regional, and above all of individual persons who compose these social groups, are made known (it is the function of *consilium* in the Thomist psychology of human acts) to the organs of government which have the duty to make the final practical decision and to exercise *imperium*, and which are free from every preoccupation save that of the common good.

society would embody distinct and compact social groups, be they called corporations or gilds or what you will. But each of these lesser unities in the social order would have its own spontaneous life not derived from the State. Thus, in the economic sphere each group would exist as a moral person made up of those who, as manual or intellectual workers or lenders of capital, collaborate in one organic task, these moral persons being endowed with as much autonomy as the organisation of the social whole will allow, and thus being something entirely separate from the public services of the State. In this conception, which avoids *étatisme* as much as possible, the organic City would be ruled not by the wheels of a bureaucratic machine but by decisions taken by men chosen as leaders of their several organisations and having in their respective ranks all the privileges and all the obligations of responsible office.[1]

It is in this sense that we called it above a society of *authoritative* type ; we might have said of aristocratic type if the operation of the law of association of ideas did not involve the risk that the words might be understood in a sense other than the sense intended. The society of which we speak would in effect be a society *sans classes*, that is to say one in which the distinctions between classes which have been heretofore observed in our Western

[1] In connexion with the problem of supreme political control we think that the advantages of heredity which were emphasized by Pascal and had been described by St. Thomas as accidental, and which chiefly concern stability in the exercise of authority, should give way in historical conditions where efficiency counts for more even than stability to those which attend the selection, by the appropriate organs in the community, of the man who will be the director-in-chief of the common good.

civilisation would have disappeared, such distinctions having been founded in earlier times chiefly on the inheritance of blood, in modern times on the inheritance of money. But a fresh differentiation would inevitably arise in a community of human beings all of whom were alike included in the category of workers, for there is no order without diversity and inequalities of rank; and in a world where social values would depend not on birth or on riches but on work, the chiefs whom the social organs of the several grades would single out would form a true aristocracy of popular choice closely bound to the service of the community by the very object of their office, and no doubt as proud and as jealous of honour and of freedom as were the old hereditary and military aristocracies.

An oligarchy practised by a party formed into a sort of sect or ascetic brotherhood and claiming to be the incarnation of the social deity (proletariat, race, or nation) may be taken to be a caricature, imperialist or dictatorial as the case may be, of the aristocracy of popular choice of which we have been speaking, and which, in a society directed towards the autonomous freedom of human personality, would spring from the mass of the working people under the free play of institutions established on a national basis.

Work itself and the dignity of labour (which is so largely unrecognised in bourgeois society) give rise in these two types of civilisation to two sets of ideas that are essentially opposed.[1]

[1] Cf. Etienne Borne, *Travail humain et Esprit chrétien*, Courrier des Iles, no. 1 ; *Travail et Contemplation*, Esprit, no. 10.

In the one, work is the supreme value and even the end of man, who is reduced on materialist principles to terms of purely transitive activity. He is (we may say) the Personification of Slavery. In the other type of civilisation, the basis of the high worth and dignity of labour lies in the intrinsic nobility of a rational nature endowed above all else with the immanent activity of intelligence and of will and directed to a last end which is not work but spiritual perfection, the freedom of exultation or fulfilment and of autonomy. Doubtless in each case the same thing may be said : " If a man will not work, neither shall he eat." But in the one case work is conceived in its simple meaning in the image of corporal activity and the making of things ; in the other its connotation[1] extends with the aid of analogy to the services rendered to man by disinterested spiritual activity which transcends local and temporal conditions and which requires a certain degree of leisure, be it pure science or art or the contemplative life. And he who said : *Si quis non vult operari, nec manducet*[2] has also said : *Dominus ordinavit iis, qui evangelium annuntiant, de evangelio vivere.*[3] Contemplation is not work, but being of supreme benefit to the community it possesses in an eminent degree the utility that gives work its value. Contemplation is not work, it is fruition, and under one form or another, in a diffuse or in a concentrated state (for words being the playthings of

---

[1] It is noteworthy that in the text to which allusion is made, St. Paul uses not *laborare*, but *operari* (ἐργάζεσθαι), a term whicn covers every human activity.
[2] St. Paul, 2 Thessalonians, iii. 10.
[3] St. Paul, 1 Cor., ix. 14.

specialists, its range is much wider than the word *contemplation* would appear to indicate), it will be found to be bound up with the achievement by the soul of its freedom of autonomy. For this reason the wisdom that goes with contemplation, whose beginnings are in lowly places but whose peaks are known only to the saints, is rightfully entitled to the highest place in our scale of values. If it is proper for some to devote themselves to it in a special way, all have none the less a spiritual call to it in greater or lesser measure even as all have a social call to work; and all have the right to be allowed to share in some way the goods that wisdom dispenses. The week of human toil should issue in the rest of God. It is not the leisure of a few lovers of plain chant but the life of the mass of the people and the whole range of social action and the common works of men that should be crowned with fêtes and liturgies and hymns and canticles.

As to the third characteristic that we have mentioned, by *pluralist* we intend a society in which, in contrast with the strict unitary conception which has been the fashion since the Renaissance, the State shall unite in a vital and not in a mechanical order legislative organs of several different kinds and social institutions of varying legal status. In the Middle Ages this pluralism was manifested in a special way by the multiplicity and sometimes by the confusion of jurisdictions and by differences of customary law. Nowadays the matter must be looked at from a different angle. We have in mind not only claims for regional autonomy which are legitimate only to the extent to which they do not involve the risk of sacrifice of political ideas and interests of a higher order to regional claims and interests. We have chiefly in mind an organic heterogeneity in the structure of civil society, in institutions and organs, for example, of the economic and also of the juridical order.

It seems to us then that in a society which would conform to the concrete historical ideal which now engages our attention, the frame and constitution of industrial life would be fundamentally different from that of agriculture. In the first case (that is, in industry) the conditions of production require a certain measure of collectivisation[1] which bursts the cadres of family economy. In the capitalist régime an industrial undertaking is a hive of salaried workers and of associated capital, in whose service the workers are ; and the more the undertaking develops by the use of machinery and the rationalisation of work, and the mobilisation of finance, the more this tendency to collectivisation becomes accentuated. To bring things back to an order more in harmony with justice, the governing rules of the industrial economy ought to subordinate this collectivist movement to the interests of human personality and the common good. Such a measure of control leads, we think, to a system in which the property in the undertaking and in the means of production passes not indeed to the State or to the nation but to corporate bodies composed of workers, technicians, and shareholders, viewed as moral persons ; so that a system of co-ownership is sub-

[1] At any rate beyond a certain limit that the use of machinery makes it easy to exceed.

stituted for the employment of workers at a wage and so that money invested on a basis of partnership and not of money-lending shall be subordinate and not superior to human values ; and so that the servitude that follows the use of the machine shall be offset by admitting the workers to share in the direction and the administration of the collective undertaking.

On the other hand the governing rules of the agricultural economy—which, be it observed, is more fundamental than the economy of the industrial order and whose welfare, in a normal society, should first be assured—ought, using modern forms and taking advantage of the benefits of machinery and of corporative organisation, to tend to the restoration and the reinforcement of family economy and of family and peasant ownership.

The same pluralist principles would find quite other opportunities of application in the order of juridical and of social institutions. To one who meditates on the problems raised by diversities of religious profession in the midst of the same civilisation, and on the possibility of finding a reasonable and pacific solution for these problems, it appears that one day the legislature may be induced in *mixed questions* (matters that have at once and inseparably a civil and a religious aspect) to concede to the several religious bodies within the State a separate legal constitution. The ethical system of an atheist is different from that of a Christian : and his capacities and his ideal in social behaviour are likewise different. In sound philosophy no doubt the atheist ethic is not the true ethic. But ought not the legislator, whose duty is to aim at the common good and at the peace of the people under his care, to pay heed to actual facts and accordingly invoke the principle of lesser evil ?[1] In certain typical instances St. Louis (whatever may have been the intrinsic worth of the solutions he adopted) looked at things in this way. If religious division among the elements that compose a single civilisation in the temporal order—divisions which in an absolute sense are to be deplored but which bear witness to the wretchedness of our human lot—if such division is a fact which modern times ought to recognise, one may ask whether the principle of lesser evil does not lead to the contemplation of a State in which, in *mixed questions* of the kind we are considering, separate categories of citizens might be recognised and constituted on the basis of these divisions.

Here is a problem of peculiar importance and peculiar difficulty. It ought at any rate to be clearly stated.

Liberalism[2] is not merely false in theory ; it is finished in fact ; bankrupt by the turn of events. The revolutions that are happening under our eyes are social and political revolutions with a " mystical " or religious basis—whether it be a soi-disant religion which worships the State as a superior form of human personality more intimate to each citizen than he is to himself, and which claims to be theist and even Christian in character ; or whether it be

[1] Cf. St. Thomas, *Summa theol.*, i-ii, 96, 2 ; ii-ii, 10, 11.
[2] On Liberalism (in its philosophic meaning) cf. *Primauté du Spirituel*, Annexe VII ; Eng. edition " The Things that are not Caesar's " (Sheed & Ward), p. 133.

the officially atheist and materialist anti-religion of the Social Commonwealth which worships Work as the supreme expression of the freedom and the power of man. Those who, because they prefer authentic spiritual values to all else, are unable to accept the one or the other of these are none the less able without displeasure to watch the crumbling of the old errors of Liberalism. For all that, they are not content to substitute for the error of Liberalism an opposite error and to erect, although only by way of aspiration and in the ideal order, a Theocratic Church in opposition to or alongside the theocracies of the Collectivist Man. They recognise the necessity of taking count of the religious divisions that the passage and the tricks of time have inscribed in the history of the world. Without inclining towards ' Dogmatic Tolerance ' which considers freedom to err as a thing good in itself, they know of what value for human personality is a true Civil Tolerance which imposes a respect for Conscience upon the State. Moreover, the more fully they realise the true significance of the age of culture that is opening before us and of its opposition to the humanism of the last four centuries, the less are they inclined to think that the new age will find in human means, least of all in the means at the disposal of the State, the equipment that is needed for the perfection of the spiritual life of man on earth.

In order to give play in fancy to their historical ideal, they must conceive a Christian or true humanist civilisation free at one and the same time from Liberalism and from Clericalism, a civilisation which is essentially religious and Christian and in which the temporal power is confessedly religious and Christian, though it does not attempt by the means of coercion at its command to impose any standard of religious conformity. In such a community the pluralist solution of which we have spoken assumes its full significance.[1] In no way does it signify that in virtue of a right in its citizens to teach and propagate any opinion whatever, the State would be obliged to give legal sanction to the constitution worked out by each spiritual group for itself in conformity with its own principles. That would be to interpret the solution in the sense of theological liberalism.[2] Understood in its proper sense the solution which is offered means that in order to avoid greater evils (that is to say, the ruin of the peace of the community and the hardening or the weakening of consciences) the State can and ought in the actual circumstances of our time to tolerate within it modes of worship that diverge to a greater or lesser extent from the true worship[3] ; and that it may accordingly decide to grant to the

[1] One recalls the formula attributed by Montalembert to the Catholic opponents of liberalism and that Jules Ferry later attributed (mistakenly) to Veuillot : " When I am the weaker, I claim freedom from you since it is your principle ; when I am the stronger, I take it from you, since that is my principle." No one assuredly professes such a doctrine. If one is to make sure, however, of being no party to it without falling into the error of Montalembert himself, in order in other words to effect a real reconciliation between non-Liberalism and Liberty and not to rest in the use of expedients or in the order of intention only, it is, we think, difficult to avoid recourse to a solution of the pluralist type that is sketched here.
[2] Hindu law seems to be inspired by the principles of such liberalism. Cf. J. R. Gharpuré, *Hindu Law*, 4th edition, Bombay, 1931.
[3] Cf. St. Thomas, *Summa theol.*, ii-ii, 10, 11 (*ritus infidelium sunt tolerandi*).

different spiritual groups that live within its borders constitutions or charters that it will adapt on the one hand to the condition of each group and on the other hand to the general tenor of its legislation in the direction of right living, and to the requirements of the moral law of which it should save all it can and to the full realisation of which it should direct as far as possible the whole series of these constitutions.[1]

We know that the State as such has duties towards God and that it ought to collaborate effectively with the Church. But the manner in which it discharges these duties may vary with historical circumstances and material conditions and must be adjusted to the dictates of reason. One may conceive two typically different modes of collaboration between the two powers. In the one case collaboration may be made effective by prominent use of the visible and external means that are proper to the temporal power, and finally by the use of force in its different manifestations. In the other case, collaboration will

---

[1] Thus for Catholics civil legislation might coincide or converge towards the Canon Law, and the pluralist structure of the State would be oriented even on the lowest levels towards the perfection of Christian law. Now let us take, at the other end of the scale, a case involving problems of colonisation, the case for example of polygamous customs in the Cameroons. If it is true that the colonising power may not impose on the natives, without introducing greater evils, the Christian law of monogamy, it is equally true that while recognising the " fetishist " and Mohammedan marriage it ought not only, as convert natives grow more and more numerous, to recognise in their case also the Christian law (which it does not yet do), but it ought also to orientate the personal law of fetishists and Mohammedans in the direction of true moral and social principles, by limiting by positive prescriptions the ravages of polygamy and by promoting at the same time everything that tends to an improvement in morals.

proceed with the use as principal means of the moral and spiritual activities that are proper to the Church, and primarily the power of Christian Charity.

It was in the natural course and in conformity with our mental structure as rational animals, for whom external signs and the objective order have a primary value, that the first of these modes of collaboration should in the order of history have been the first to be attempted. It brought enduring benefits and led also to great abuses. The most extreme of its forms of error appear in certain types of civilisation (such as the Puritan type) in which the power of the State is linked to forms of religious organisation emptied of their spiritual content and become simply vegetative. It is to the credit of ancient Christendom that an injury done to the common good of the temporal order in its subordination to eternal values was felt to be of its nature a graver hurt than a more obvious wrong that affected it only in the order of temporal things. In one sense a State which was prepared to inflict death for the crime of heresy showed a greater concern for the good of souls and a nobler conception of the dignity of human society (thus centred on truth) than a State which only punishes for crimes committed against the body. It being assumed I am to be punished, you honour me more in my character as a rational being by burning me for my ideas than by hanging me or guillotining me for an act of my hands. In truth, however, mankind has had enough experience of that way of paying homage to the rational being of man : and it will be easy to understand if man should elect in future to decline the honour.

It is, we think, the second of the contrasted modes of collaboration of Church and State, with the advantages and also the disadvantages proper to it, that a Christian or truly humanist civilisation would be expected in our time to use. And the conception that would inspire it would be noble also and worthy of man : but, history having turned on its axis, another hemisphere of the metaphysical firmament with other constellations would appear above. A State which, without recognising any right in heresy as such, assures to the heretic his liberties as a citizen and even grants him a juridical status adapted to his ideas and his moral habits— not only because it wishes to avoid civil discord but also because it respects and protects his human nature and the reserves of spiritual power that inhabit the souls of men and that of a sinner may make a saint, and of an infidel may make a Christian, in a word because a Christian love of rational beings makes it prefer mercy to justice[1]—such a State promotes the spiritual life of its citizens *on the objective side* much less than a less tolerant State would do. The level of wisdom and of virtue below which the body social will not tolerate evil or error is definitely lowered, though less so of course than in the neutral State of Liberal philosophy. But the State of which we are now thinking gives more encouragement to the spiritual life of its citizens *on the subjective side*, their right to claim the

[1] " *Misericordiam volo, et non sacrificium.*" Osee, vi. 6 ; Matt. xi. 13.

68

privilege of extra-territoriality against the temporal power on the ground of Conscience (which is capable of being illuminated from within by the Maker of the Universe) being carried to a higher level. And it is also clear that the interests of a durable social peace in a community which admits diversity of religious profession require that the collaboration of Church and State be effected by way of moral influence and amity rather than by legal constraint.[1]

In such a case the State does not enforce by its proper organs or by force the privileges to which the true religion has a right—at the hazard of being treated as one of these organs.[2] But it encourages and expressly facilitates the expansion of the proper uses and energies of religion[3]; and, following the

---

[1] Cf. Cardinal Manning's reply to Mr. Gladstone : " If Catholics were in power to-morrow in England, not a penal law would be proposed, nor the shadow of constraint be put upon the faith of any man. We would that all men fully believed the truth ; but a forced faith is a hypocrisy hateful to God and man. . . . If the Catholics were to-morrow the ' Imperial race ' in these Kingdoms they would not use political power to molest the divided and hereditary religious state of our people. We would not shut one of their Churches, or Colleges, or Schools. They would have the same liberties we enjoy as a minority." *The Vatican Decrees*, London, 1875, pp. 93-94.

[2] In the concordats of the period of the Renaissance and the Empire, the State while remunerating the clergy as its own officials reserved to itself certain prerogatives, in particular, the choice of bishops. If a type of lay Christian State such as that we are contemplating were to arise, perhaps the future would bring arrangements of a different type, in which the Church and the State would agree on the best method of mutual aid and collaboration for the welfare of the mass of citizens, without any provision for the remuneration of the Clergy by the State and without any interference by the State in the government of the Church.

[3] As regards instruction, for example, the claim for what is now called " la proportionnelle scolaire " is in the line of colla-boration indicated here. One sees why a *neutral* State and a Totalitarian State are opposed to it in principle. The educational régime that M. Dielininkaitis in his thesis on *La Liberté scolaire*

principles of the *jus amicabile*, the State in turn is able to enlist in its favour the wisdom, the virtue, the mystical stores that religion dispenses to peoples and to governors, the privileges of true religion being chiefly asserted through its own pre-eminence in spiritual efficacy.

On a later page will be found some reflexions on the idea of a lay Christian State which we think it is as important to define as the notion of Christian philosophy.[1] The observations we have just made may serve in some measure to illustrate the idea we have in mind.

A similar question arises in relation to the measure of moral and spiritual unity that is requisite for the formation and maintenance of a civilisation. The diversity of legal constitutions and the pluralist structure of the Christian civilisation of which we have given here an ideal outline do indeed relax and distend this unity but they do not destroy it. Here again old truths must be understood in a new setting. The unity of such a civilisation no longer appears as a unity of an essential or constitutional

---

de l'Etat calls " régimes de liberté scolaire par l'Etat " seems on the other hand to contemplate a Christian State in the conditions of the modern world ; it being clearly understood that one is dealing not with a right that any sect could claim, but with a problem of fact in the solution of which political wisdom is entitled to impose reasonable limits and to secure the most favourable orientation.

[1] Can philosophy be specifically Christian ? The matter has been much discussed in a recent controversy. See *De la Philosophie Chrétienne* by M. Maritain ; *L'Esprit de la Philosophie Médiévale* by M. Gilson (Vol. II, p. 289-290) ; *Ya-t-il une philosophie Chrétienne ?* by M. Bréhier, Revue de Métaphysique et de la Morale, April, 1931 ; *Le Problème de la Philosophie Catholique*, by M. Blondel ; *De la Philosophie Chrétienne* by A. D. Sertillanges, O.P.,in *La Vie Intellectuelle*, 10 Oct., 1933.

character guaranteed from above by the profession of the same doctrine and the same faith. Though the unity is less perfect, and material rather than formal in character, it is none the less real ; it is a unity of Becoming or of orientation which springs from a common aspiration and gathers elements of heterogeneous culture (of which some may indeed be very imperfect) into a form of civilisation which is fully consonant with the eternal interests of human personality and with man's freedom of autonomy.

I who am a Catholic understand and appreciate that the momentum of such a movement carries it towards a Catholic form of civilisation ; and I know that to maintain its course it has need of the Wisdom that goes with Catholicism. But then it is proper to this wisdom to direct civilisation not by imposing its conceptions authoritatively from above because they are Catholic, but by demonstrating experimentally as it were from below that they are conformable to right reason and to the common good ; a proof that the strength of prejudice and the blindness of many make difficult but not impossible. Is it not true that in our time the teaching of the Roman Pontiffs tends to be accepted as a beacon light not by Catholics only but by all men of good will ? Such proof as we have in mind, however, would be above all a practical and experimental proof made in the order of political reality, by men whose energy and ability would have marked them out for power.

A temporal order of this kind in which the moral and spiritual unity of the State is not suppressed but relaxed and (so to say) distended, would belong in substance to the political order directed (according to the Aristotelian division) rather by an ideal of civic freedom than by an ideal of virtue or of unity. It would belong, that is to say, to a democratic order (in the sense of Aristotle, not of Rousseau)[1] notwithstanding the prominence given by way of balance to the element of authority we have already mentioned. In short, one would have in this conception of the State a type of mixed régime in which would be found united and tempered one by another the three forms of government that classical politics have distinguished.[2] But while the *régime mixte* of medieval France was a monarchy with aristocratic and democratic elements, the mixed régime we are now considering would be better described as a democracy with aristocratic and monarchical elements, these expressions being taken (let me repeat) in the philosophic and Aristotelian sense in which the schoolmen understood them and not in the mythical and emotional sense they have been given in the language of modern democracy.

We are aware that in contradistinction to the philosophical theses and principles that have been stated in the earlier pages of this essay many of the opinions we have offered in this final section are matters of conjecture. We have thought it right, however, to give expression to these conjectures, for practical philosophy has not to do only with the

[1] Cf. *Three Reformers*, pp. 126-140.
[2] Cf. Marcel Demongeot, *Le meilleur régime politique selon saint Thomas*, Paris, Blot, 1927 (especially Part II, chapters III and IV) ; see also *The Things that are not Caesar's*, appendix 6.

certainties of universal and necessary law. Its function is also, with the instruments of probability and hypothesis and anticipation, to approach and make contact with the world of contingent reality in which those laws are realised.

RELIGION AND CULTURE

RELIGION AND CULTURE

I

ON THE IDEA OF ORDER

Of the philosophy of St. Thomas it is not possible
to say, as Berdyaev said of the types of philosophy
developed in the course of history under the influence
of the Orthodox Church, that the concept of order
is alien to it. On the contrary, this concept plays
in the philosophy of St. Thomas a rôle so universal
and so deep that we are put on our guard against any
over-simple treatment of the problems in which it
arises.

The idea of order is close to that of unity, which
means that it belongs to the domain of the transcendentals[1] and is capable of realisation on different
planes and in different degrees. It would be a
prime disorder not to accept the hierarchy of the
different orders ; and to attenuate the idea of order
by considering it only in its lesser analogies.

Order is itself, like Being, a good. But it is
not the absolute good. There is order in hell.
External and visible order is ordained to inner and
invisible order. The order of bodies subserves
that of soul or Spirit, and this latter subserves

---

[1] The transcendentals are Unity, Truth, Goodness, Beauty.
(Tr.).

the order of Charity. But there is no necessary correspondence between these orders ; he who is of higher rank in the ecclesiastical hierarchy is not necessarily of higher rank in the order of sanctity.

The order of good moral and civil administration prescribes that publicans[1] and prostitutes shall take rank after persons of honourable life. The order of the Kingdom of Heaven permits publicans and prostitutes to take rank, in the inscrutable judgment of God, before persons of honourable life.

We shall not deal with order that is false or of pure appearance : the order of tyranny (*ubi solitudinem faciunt* . . .), which is a caricature of civil order ; the rules of academies, which are a counterfeit of the laws of poetry. There is an order that is mechanical and coercive ; and an order that is natural and spontaneous ; and again an order that is vital and organic. There is an order of necessity and an order of freedom. There is an order of nature and an order of grace ; there is an order of reason and an order of Charity. Under the order of the old law the main thing was the written word ; under the order of the new law it is the grace of the Holy Spirit.[2]

The " objective order that is imposed on man " is in a general way that of the natures of things with their respective laws (and first and foremost human nature) and the order of truth and of supernatural life : it flows from the Eternal law which is the wisdom of the Maker of all things. And it is imposed on man by being expressed in his reason

[1] In the sense of the Scriptures. (Tr.)
[2] *Summa theol.*, i-ii, 106, 1.

78

and in his conscience through vital entry and incorporation in his immanent activities of knowing and willing. It is a vital act to adhere to that which is and to acknowledge by our mind and will an order that we did not create.

Force is necessary in civil communities because of men who are violent and inclined to vice[1] but it has a pedagogic office and ought to lead in the direction of freedom. It is only a substitute for those creations of freedom that we call virtues. The good man like the Prince[2] has no contact with the bloody hand of the law ; he knows only its kind eyes, for he fulfils the law not out of compulsion but out of love and of his own free will, *voluntarius non coactus*.

THE MAKING OF ORDER

It is proper here to add that reason has to do more than to recognise the order that issues from the Creative Mind. There is an order that it is the office of reason, as practical reason, to make : it is, to be exact, the order of human acts and operations which (in the teaching of St. Thomas) defines the field of ethics. Continuing and collaborating with the Divine action, reason has at every moment to fashion in conformity with the Eternal order the contingent and perpetually renewed order of the

[1] " Sed quia inveniuntur quidam protervi, et ad vitia proni, qui verbis de facili moveri non possunt, necessarium fuit quod per vim et metum cohibentur a malo, ut saltem sic malefacere desistentes, et aliis quietam vitam redderent, et ipsi tandem, per hujusmodi assuetudinem ad hoc perducerentur, quod voluntarie facerent quae prius metu implebant, et sic fierent virtuosi." *Summa theol.*, i-ii, 95, 1.
[2] Cf. *Summa theol.*, i-ii, 96, 5. ad 3.

works of time : *facere veritatem*, in the Gospel phrase.

In this way to the natural law[1] reason adds the determinations of positive law ; in this way are established organs of civil society which is indeed prescribed by nature and necessarily presupposes certain laws of nature but which is the work of reason and of virtue and has in Justice " the mystical basis of its authority." So that the words that so many men intent on establishing order repeat after Goethe, " I prefer injustice to disorder," are in truth a mere slogan of anarchy and disorder.

The whole order of human life is not ready-made in nature and in things ; it is an Order of Freedom ; it has not just to be discovered and accepted : it has also to be made.

And here the study of things past and of the process by which things come to be assumes its full importance. Truly, History is not the Eternal Gospel ; it is not the Absolute. Becoming is no more Eternal law than Time is God. But it is in the process of becoming and in the ceaseless change of things that the building of order is laid on us as an obligation. And the tragedy of our situation (it is not true tragedy for it has a divine ending) is that we have to grope at our work, overwhelmed by the darkness that obscures our past, humbled by it in our very intelligence which in a sense indeed makes history, yet whose knowledge is all but limited to things that have just happened before our eyes.

It is disorder dearly bought to despise the Eternal

---

[1] The Natural Law is defined : *participatio legis aeternae in rationali creatura.*

order and to look forward to a new order which shall arise out of the mere surge of Becoming and the mere movement of history, an order accomplished and precipitated by those who know the secrets of history, the Levites of the revolutionary process, the elect of the god of Immanence in whom the *Weltgeist* becomes conscious of itself. But it is disorder equally serious to forget that the order of human affairs is made in the making of history and that if it is to be what it ought to be it must be continuously created by ceaseless effort of reason and of will, of imagination and of virtue, rescuing from the evil of the time and fashioning with the tools that are at hand things consonant with the temporal and the eternal good of human beings. From this point of view certain instances of obvious disorder, of overthrow and of destruction, may represent the elimination in the process of history of deeper and less obvious disorder—and the price that has to be paid for the misdeeds and omissions of those who forget that justice is, in the language of St. Catherine of Siena, the sentinel of States.

Lastly, if it be true that the first thing necessary is to establish order within us, because every commencement is from within, the first condition of work for the establishment of a true order will be an entire subordination of the soul to truth. In its office for Good Friday, when the Church beseeches God to take away the evils that oppress the world, it is *of every error* that she first begs deliverance ; *Oremus Deum patrem omnipotentem ut cunctis mundum purget erroribus ; morbos auferat : famem depellat . . .*

True principles and ardent generosity are apt to prove sterile if the soul is not delivered into the fulness of truth. If it is riveted at a single point to false or narrow judgments, its vision of the detail of facts and events will be deformed and its desire for true order will fail to be translated into reality. Integrity is essential to order.

II

ON HUMANISM

The problem of Humanism is often put in inacurate terms, for the reason no doubt that on the one hand Humanism retains a certain affinity with the naturalist currents of the Renaissance and on the other hand the Christian idea is contaminated in the mind of many of us by traces of Jansenism or of Puritanism.

The quarrel is not between Humanism and Christianity.

It is between two several conceptions of Humanism. For if it is true that culture is " the expansion of the peculiarly human life, including not only whatever material development may be necessary and sufficient to enable us to lead an upright life on this earth, but also and above all moral development of the speculative and practical activities (artistic and ethical) peculiarly worthy of being called a human development,"[1] then to speak of culture or civilisation is to speak of the common good of

[1] *Religion et Culture*, English edition, pp. 6-7.

human beings in the terrestrial or the temporal
order. In the sense of our definition there is no
culture that is not humanist. An essentially anti-
humanist philosophy would involve an absolute
condemnation of culture or of civilisation. Such
is perhaps the tendency of the ultra-calvinist theology
of persons like Karl Barth. But this absolute
condemnation of human values is Manichean and
non-Christian ; it is incompatible with the central
truth of Christianity, the dogma of the Incarnation.

The debate that divides our contemporaries and
that compels us all to make an election is between
two conceptions of Humanism : a *theocentric*
conception, which is the Christian conception ; and
an *anthropocentric* conception, which has its first
origins in the spirit of the Renaissance. The first
(theocentric) conception may be described as
authentic Humanism ; the second (anthropocentric)
conception may be called inhuman Humanism.

It must always be understood that the *theocentric*
or authentic Humanism of which we speak is something wholly different from the " Christian Humanism " or Christian naturalism that began to flourish
in the sixteenth century and of which the world has
had enough to make it sick and tired—of which
indeed even God is sick and tired, for it is of just
that kind of Humanism that He is now engaged in
making an end. St. Thomas Aquinas and St. John
of the Cross are the great doctors of authentic
Humanism which is of service to man and to human
interests just because it will tolerate no attenuation
of divine truth and because it disposes the whole
man to the Folly of the Cross and to the mystery

83

of the redeeming Blood. Its pattern is the image of a man, a King clothed in scarlet and crowned with thorns and bleeding at every pore ; *Behold the Man ; He hath borne our infirmities*. It is to Him that men are conformed by grace, being made partakers of the divine nature and by adoption sons of God, destined at the end of their spiritual development to become gods by participation of the divine life, when Charity will have accomplished its work of melting their hearts. And it is by being conformed in this way to their Redeemer and Lord that they enter in their turn into the mystery of His redemptive action, consummating through the whole range of time—by way of experience, though not by way of merit—what was wanting to His suffering. If fallen nature inclines overmuch to understand the word Humanism in its anthropocentric meaning it is all the more important to disentangle the true notion and the true conditions of the only Humanism that does not make havoc of human nature ; and for this reason to break with the spirit of the Renaissance.

ON AMBIVALENCE IN HISTORY

To denounce a fundamental spiritual deviation in a period of culture is not to condemn that period. One does not pass judgment on history. It would be about as sensible for a Christian to condemn modern times as it would be for rationalists (nor do they altogether miss the opportunity) to condemn the Middle Ages.

An error in spiritual principle bears its inevitable fruit. We must expose the principle and avow the loss. During the same period there is an evolution in human affairs, an expansion of history ; there are, conjoined to certain evils, gains and achievements of mankind that have an almost sacred value since they are produced in the order of divine providence ; we must acknowledge these attainments and these gains.

And here arises a serious question which we venture to call the question of the Evil One as an actor in history.

St. Gregory wrote : " Men should know that the will of Satan is always unrighteous but that his power is never unjust," for " the iniquities he proposes to commit God allows in all justice."[1] This saying goes a long way. It supplies an important principle of historical exegesis.

The devil hangs like a vampire on the side of history. History moves forward none the less and moves forward with the vampire. It is only in the Church as Church that the devil has no place. He takes part in the onward march of the world and in a sense instigates it. His chief activity is to do in his particular way (which is not a good way) what good folk omit to do, because they are asleep. That which is done is done badly, but it is done.

The Prince of this world takes possession of the things of time as far as these things are not redeemed by the blood of Christ. But time belongs to God : it is He who first wills movement and change. There is a passage full of strange meaning in the

[1] P.L. LXXV. 564.

85

Hymn of Habacuc, in the Vulgate. It is there said that the devil goes before the feet of God : *et egredietur diabolus ante pedes ejus.* He runs before Him : as a traitor he prepares His ways.

Truth to tell, history is bicephalous. The head of all the good folk leads his party to the place where God will be all in all ; the head of all the wicked leads his party to the place where the creature will be all things to itself. When the members of these two parties who at every instant are intermingled shall have finally separated, history itself will be at an end.

A MANICHEAN CONCEPTION OF HISTORY

The rationalists are driven to a sort of Manichean conception of history which Christian thought avoids.

When the first and fundamental measure by which all else is measured, when the prime Good, that is to say, is something in the human order, this Good will have an opposite ; and this opposite, being opposed to the Good, can only have the office of pure evil.

If the primary good is political liberty, the principles of 1789, there will be in history elements of pure darkness : the " tyranny " that is opposed to this liberty.

If the primary Good is Cartesian thinking, there will be ages and philosophies assigned to utter darkness of which the progress of thought can hope for no good result. If the primary good is Becoming, in the sense of History, there will

86

again be elements utterly hateful : those that refuse to march in step with History.

That is why in all these cases the struggle is so bitter : it is always the old struggle of Ormuzd against Ahriman.

The Christian for his part knows that God has no opposite. For the Christian indeed there is also a struggle between light and darkness, between truth and error ; but in existing reality there cannot be *pure* darkness, or *pure* error, because all that is, in the measure in which it is, is of God. In the thought of the atheist, or, if you prefer, of the enemy of God, as Proudhon nominated himself, it is impossible that God be at the service of the enemy of God ; whilst in the thought of the Christian the enemy of God is at the service of God. God has his adversaries, not in the metaphysical but in the moral order. Yet his adversaries are always at His service. He is served by the martyrs, and by the executioners who made them martyrs. Everything that happens in the history of the world serves in one way or another the progress of the Church and, in a more or less obscure way, some kind of progress of the world. This line of thought is apt to enlarge our horizon in a notable way.

Voltaire, setting out to crush the Beast (*écraser l'infâme*), was in Christendom and in the history of Christendom what he was in the created universe and in the order of Providence. He served them in spite of himself. His campaign for tolerance, though a fight for one error (since it is absurd, as Saint-Simon and Auguste Comte saw clearly, to exalt freedom of thought to an absolute end without any law higher than subjective opinion), led him at the same time to fight against another error not less evil in its effect : I mean the modern error, which has found expression in the formula *cujus regio ejus religio*, that the force of the State and social pressure have of their own nature a right to control Conscience. In this respect Voltaire was striving without knowing it for Article 1351 of the Code of Canon Law : " No one shall be compelled to embrace the Catholic Faith against his Will."

The Christian thus possesses knowledge of an intuitive kind which enables him with more peace of heart than has the follower of Spinoza, to see all things *sub specie aeterni*. I find a symbol of this spiritual universality in a book by G. K. Chesterton, *The Man who was Thursday*, where one is shown the police and the anarchists (who fight one another conscientiously) obedient to the same mysterious lord whom the author calls Mr. Sunday.

THE TEMPTATION OF HISTORY

One who makes it his first principle to advance with the times or to make the times advance, and to march in step, binds himself in so doing to collaborate with all the agents of change. He lands himself in very mixed company.

We are not co-operators with change ; we are co-operators with God.

To absent oneself from history is to seek death. Eternity does not vacate time ; but possesses it from

on high. Our duty is to act on history to the limit
of our power, God being first served ; but to be
resigned if it often works against us : it will not
happen against the will of God. Thus, the chief
thing for us, from the point of view of existence
in history, is not to succeed, for success does not
endure for ever ; but to have been there, in it,
for this is indelible.

A PROBLEM FOR ANTHROPOCENTRIC HUMANISM

It is a commonplace that man is naturally a
religious animal : it is impossible to have a complete
conception of man unless we include the God whom
he adores. But, we note, as a fact, that all existing religions, and in a singular way the Judaeo-
Christian religions, which profess the dogma of
creation, subordinate the human being to a Supreme
Being on whom all things depend. If in so doing
they teach error, and one which affects the very
sources of our life, it is clearly our moral duty to
endeavour to release mankind from such error.

Now, this constitutes a problem, or rather two
major problems, for anthropocentric humanism : for
(1) it begins with a proceeding which is catastrophic
for mankind. With a view to enriching humanity,
it obliges man first of all to renounce an inheritance
with which all his history is entwined ; and (2) since
it is impossible to establish an authentic humanism
without integrating it to a religion, and since all
existing religions must by hypothesis be excluded,
it remains for the humanism of which we are speaking

to found a new religion. Auguste Comte clearly saw the necessity of it. One would like to know if the exponents in our time of humanism of a rationalist or sceptical sort have taken note of the obligation that rests upon them. If they decline the mission, one way of escape and one way only is open to them : to change the nature of man. It is the Russian solution : to create an Atheist Man. In spite of appearances, this solution is in line with the Renaissance movement. It is the normal result of a humanism *cut off* from the Incarnation, when it rids itself of all the residues of theocentric culture that it carried with it and that for a time masked and weakened its native energy. Though it marks the extreme limit of unreason the Russian solution possesses at any rate this merit, that if the Godless make war on religion, they think it false. No doubt the immediate reason is that religion prevents the proletariat from giving itself wholeheartedly to the class war. But even that supposes the ' scientific ' conviction that religion is untrue. There is thus in the last analysis, and despite the ignorance and the falsehood in which it is enveloped, a decision taken in the name of truth.

But observe the contradiction ! It is an act of religion to declare war on God. " It is so easy for a Russian to become an atheist," wrote Dostoievsky,[1] " more easy than for any other inhabitant of the globe. And our folk do not simply become atheist ; they *believe* in atheism like a new religion, without realising it is belief in Nothing."

[1] *The Idiot.* Dent's Everyman Library No. 682.

THE MYTH OF IMMANENCE

Nothing is more valuable in metaphysics than the notion of immanent activity, the mark of mind. But it is in a very different meaning that the word *immanence* is understood in current speech and that the sages of anthropocentric humanism have affirmed the principle of Immanence. This principle signifies for them that all things are contained in the heart of man and in his history. " Already amid the ruins of old beliefs, Man swears by his own humanity; he cries aloud, his left hand on his heart, his right hand stretched out to infinity : ' It is I who am King of the universe. All that is outside me is inferior to me. And I, I am subject to no Majesty.' "[1] The dependence of man in relation to material conditions which he must learn to control is of course admitted. But it is said there is no dependence that he needs to acknowledge to an order of things superior to his will or to a God who has created him. In our view it is absurd to admit dependence in one case and to deny it in the other. How could man be dependent on things of an inferior order if he were not in his essence a dependent being, and if there were not therefore something above him on which he must depend ?

The myth of Immanence is destructive of the real values of immanence, that is of mind, since these values go with the rational nature of man, that is, human *personality;* and human personality is doomed by the dialectic of pure Immanence. Sovereignty has its source in personality. But the

[1] Proudhon : *Justice*, 1st essay.

precarious and limited personality of human beings taken singly is incompatible with the absolute sovereignty that is attributed to Mankind. Of necessity therefore personality has to pass to a general or universal subject, to Collective Humanity, to Becoming or to Matter ; where it is lost and disappears.

It is only in the affirmation of Divine Transcendence and of the Incarnation that the values of immanence can be saved. A constant increase in spirituality is possible for each one until he dies, and for successive generations until the end of the world, if there is an Uncreated Spirit, Subsisting Love, to Whom each can be more and more united by advancing more and more towards sanctity, and Who pursuing the work of redemption across the ages through the body of the Church attracts to Him the rising tide in history, while the ebb tide falls and flows to its proper destination.

On the other hand, to seek spirituality either in the growth of intellectual processes, or in the technical work of improvement of the living conditions of mankind, or in an attempt to direct by human reason the forces of history, involves no increase in the existing stock of spirituality. It presupposes an accumulation of spiritual force that may be released in this way ; it involves an expenditure of spiritual energies which in truth is possible only by virtue of reserves that have previously been accumulated.

We may call attention here to a misunderstanding of enormous magnitude of which a man like Proudhon affords a typical instance. He blundered

badly about the Christian conception of transcendence ; and that not only because (like so many
Frenchmen educated in the classics) he mistook
ideas that are in reality Jansenist for truly Catholic
ideas. His mistake was rooted also in an error
on the deeper levels of philosophy. If he stuffed
the notion of Transcendence with Absolutism of
all sorts ; absolutism of the State, of the Rich,
of the Priesthood, to make them issue in the culmin-
ating Absolutism of a Celestial Tyrant, it is because
he pushed to its final conclusion, with a naiveté
equalled only (so we think) by William James, an
essentially univocal and anthropomorphic conception
of the Transcendent God. The conception he
used is in truth pure nonsense. If God is a Cause
like other causes, a Person *like* other persons, a
King *like* other kings, these terms being simply
carried to their absolute meaning, it follows that
He is an all-powerful Cause only because He uses
compulsion against every creature ; that He is
sovereign Freedom only because He determines
good and evil by an act of arbitrary will ; that
He is worthy of adoration only because He annihilates
man as he goes. All this is for us nonsense, since
it is to make created things the measure of the
Uncreated God and totally to misunderstand His
Transcendence.

God is an All-powerful Cause because He gives
to all things their being and their very nature
and acts in them, more intimate to them than they
are to themselves, in the way that is proper to
their essential being ; thus assuring from within the
free action of those creatures that are by nature free.

He is free to love or to create this or that. But Justice springs from His very Essence as He sees it in his Eternal vision and not from an act of arbitrary will. " To say that Justice depends on the mere will of God," says St. Thomas,[1] " is to say that the Divine Will does not act in accordance with the order of Divine Wisdom ; which is blasphemy." The divine Wisdom is supremely free. It is nowise despotic in its action upon created things.

And finally, far from annihilating man, God gives him existence and teaches him to be a Person before Him. It is a very significant fact that the idea of human personality and also the practical recognition of the dignity of human personality developed only during those centuries in which the dogmas of the Trinity and of the Incarnation were teaching Christendom the truths of Divine Personality.

THE DIALECTIC OF MODERN CULTURE

Criticism of the modern world ought to rest on argumentation that is at once and indissolubly *humanist* and *theocentric*.

From this point of view three aspects or ' moments' inseparably related one to another may be distinguished in what we may call the dialectic of modern culture.

One may describe the first as a reversal of the order of ends. Instead of directing its proper good, which is a good of the terrestrial order, towards Eternal life, modern civilisation seeks its last end

[1] *De Veritate*, 23. 6.

within itself ; and the end it seeks is the dominion
of man over matter. God becomes the guarantor
of this dominion.

The second ' moment ' or aspect is a semi-divine
imperialism (so to say) over material forces. Instead
of accepting natural conditions and controlling
these by a process that is itself natural and that
qualifies the interior life of man, in other words that
tends primarily to inner perfection and a certain
wisdom of soul and life, civilisation sets out to alter
the conditions of nature, to rule over it by technical
and artificial processes ; creating with the aid of the
science of mathematical physics a material world
adapted to the felicity of our earthly life. God
becomes an idea.

The third ' moment ' consists in a progressive
retirement of man before the forces of matter.
In order to rule over nature as a demiurge man
is in fact obliged more and more to subordinate his
intelligence and his life to necessities not human
but technical and to forces of the material order
that he sets in motion and that invade our human
life.—God dies : Man now materialist thinks he
can only be man or superman if God is not God.

Whatever the advantage may be from other points
of view, the actual conditions of human life are
in these ways becoming more and more inhuman.
And it is by means more and more artificial in turn
that it is sought to remedy the evils that spring
from our existing artificial ways. A certain style
of pedagogy, a certain orientation of professional
life, a certain ' scientific ' psycho-therapy are
other modes of external technique by which anthropo-

centric humanism tries in vain to react against the inevitable pursuit of freedom in a way that follows from its own principles, namely by the use of technique and not by way of asceticism. We have pointed out elsewhere that the debate between freedom by use of technique or freedom by way of asceticism is the great debate of our time. " There are two ways of conceiving the mastery of man over himself. Man can become master of his nature by imposing on the world of his own inner energies the law of reason, of reason assisted by grace. This work, which is the formation of oneself on love, requires that our branches be cut in order that we may bear fruit : which is mortification. Such a practice follows the ethics of asceticism.

" The heirs of rationalism seek to impose on us to-day an entirely different system of ethics, an anti-ascetic system that is exclusively technological. An appropriate technique ought to permit us to rationalise human life, that is, to satisfy our desires with the least possible measure of inconvenience, and without any inner reformation of our own selves."[1] I fully appreciate that it means ultimately the radical transformation of man, but always from the outside and by technical means which seem to ape the efficacy of grace. Such a system of ethics does not enfranchise man. It kills him and galvanises the corpse.

" Technique is good, machinery is good. We ought to express our disapproval of the diehard spirit that seeks to suppress machinery and technical processes. But if machinery and technical processes

[1] J. Maritain, *Le Songe de Descartes*.

are not controlled and firmly subjugated to the well-being of mankind, that is to say, fully and vigorously subordinated to the ethics of religion and made the instruments of moral asceticism, mankind is irretrievably and literally lost."

III

CULTURE AND RELIGION

From the Catholic point of view it behoves us to make a very clear distinction between culture or civilisation, which belongs to the temporal order, and religion, which belongs to the spiritual order, to the Kingdom of God. Religion has for its end eternal life and for its true corporate body the Church of Christ; and since its roots are thus plunged in the supernatural order, it is truly and entirely universal and above all distinctions of race and nation and culture.

On the other hand the different systems of culture which belong essentially to the natural and temporal order are incomplete and all of them imperfect. No system of civilisation has clean hands.

It is of the highest importance to recognise the distinction between these two orders and the independence of the spiritual in relation to the cultural order. In our days the type and pattern of the kind of problem that is governed by this distinction is to be seen in missionary activity. The Church is not willing at any price to be enlisted in the work of colonisation by any Power, for such

97

work belongs to the order of civilisation or of culture. She meets opposition on this score not only at the hands of governments but also on the part of many Catholics who are badly educated in these matters and whose thought of the contemporary world is conditioned by a mass of fictitious images which represent a degenerate form of cultural ethic that was proper to the period of the Crusades. The right distinction must here be made between Catholics and Catholicism.

DANGERS ARISING FROM TEMPORAL FORMS OF SPIRITUAL THINGS

The word Christendom relates to the cultural order. It denotes a certain temporal régime that is common to peoples educated by the Church.[1] There is only one Church; there may be divers types of Christian civilisation, different expressions of ' Christendom.'

This essential distinction goes much further than is often thought. Since medieval culture had been formed by Christianity and was deeply impregnated with its spirit, and since the temporal power itself took a ministerial part in the sacred office, the distinction between the two orders, between the things of God and the things of Caesar,

[1] No doubt the word ' Christendom ' can also denote in this way the cultural and temporal radiation of the Church only by connoting the Church itself which is the source of this radiation. It is of importance none the less to mark more clearly than was done of old that it refers directly not to the Church but to divers temporal formations that arise under her influence, and on this point to keep our vocabulary particularly strict and clear.

held good in theory ; but in reality a dissociation
between the two orders was practically impossible.
This was, of itself, a great good.   To this substantial
good, however, was annexed a danger such as is
easily discernible even now in certain countries
with a long tradition ; infiltration of sociological
values into the spiritual order.   Temporal values
were consecrated by the spiritual as the Emperor
was consecrated by the Pope.   But by a reflex
movement that it is easy to understand, these same
institutions aspired to be treated as truly spiritual
values, even as the Emperor dared to claim to dictate
to the Church.[1]

It is easy to see the affinity which this dangerous
divergence has with the error we have called
Imperialism in spiritualibus and which consists
in confounding the Catholic religion with the
culture of Catholic peoples; in treating the Kingdom
of God as if it were a terrestrial city or a terrestrial
civilisation and then claiming for it and for divine
truth the same kinds of triumph as we do for a city
or a civilisation of the purely temporal order.

That which was a danger in the Middle Ages
and then gave rise to serious abuses (though never

---

[1] For instance it was common in the Middle Ages to speak of
the University of Paris as an essential organ of the Catholic
Church.   The Chronicle of Jourdain ranked it from this point
of view immediately alongside the Priesthood and the Empire.
As M. Gilson says (*Vigile*, 1st cahier, 1931, p. 68), " This way
of talking is characteristic of the state of medieval Europe and
of the illusory hopes it fostered.   One may observe at this period
a strong inclination to identify the Church with the City of
God, and Christendom with the Church as if things of the
historical and temporal order were already wholly reabsorbed
in the spirituality of its end.   Cf. *L'Eglise et la Civilisation
au Moyen Age* by Gustave Schnürer.

99

in essential matters) was destined to become a scourge that grew more and more menacing as Christian civilisation declined and religion itself became enfeebled in the hearts of many who for reasons of education or of family tradition continued in the social following of a faith that had no longer any meaning for their interior life.

During the bourgeois period of our civilisation a religion *naturalised* in this way penetrated our culture and our social order so as to form part of it and became one of the elements that the governing classes needed to enable them to govern properly. " The people must have a religion " : this formula expressed in an exact though inverted form the same conception as the phrase of Marx that religion is the opium of the people. Atheist communism is only bourgeois deism turned the other way round.

THE CHURCH AND THE CHRISTIAN WORLD

This pathological process has been in operation a considerable time. One may now hope that the end is near.

In the last century the Catholic Church, whose business is to maintain the deposit of truth, took the initiative (it was her primary duty) by denouncing the false metaphysics from which the opponents of the old order drew their energy and their passion. Hence the Syllabus and the condemnation of the different forms of liberalism. These acts of condemnation were for Catholics a definitive statement of truths of capital importance. Not that the

Church has condemned the modern world or the new age, for such words have no meaning : She made a beginning by purifying the domain of thought and by eliminating error.

Again, out of the duty of protection she owed to a multitude of souls and also out of loyalty to temporal forms that (in spite of many acts of resistance and sometimes of oppression) had served her in her spiritual ministry through long centuries of time, the Church, while struggling against the existing abuses, attempted to support as long as they had any life in them types of social structure that had been inherited from the Christian past and that had endured the test of time.

But when life, which means above all the sanctity of justice, fades completely from such institutions, a moment comes when nature herself repeats the words of the Gospel : let the dead bury their dead.

Catholicism will always maintain the principles and the truths that govern every type of civilisation and will always lend its protection to all that in the existing order continues true to these principles. But it seems now to be setting its course in the direction of new cultural types.

The time would seem to have come for Christianity to draw its full consequences from the fact that the world which issued from the Renaissance and the Reformation has completed its process of separation from Christ. For Christianity can own no fellowship with the principles of putrefaction which are at work in a world that one may fairly take to be the corpse of medieval Christendom.

If in the course of this decline of Christendom

a contingent bond happened to unite what may not be called religion but rather a certain sociological projection of religion and a class whose material interests it served (making mockery of the sacred word that was spoken in honour of Poverty : " the Poor you always have with you "), this bond is now broken. Catholicism, which is endeavouring to restore the perennial philosophy (*philosophia perennis*), is working also to restore an *oeconomia perennis* which shall serve human and not material ends and which shall be intrinsically subordinated to ethics ; and again a theory of politics which shall maintain a *communal* and *personal* conception of civilisation and the State ; and a sociology which, while admitting that the appropriation by man of material goods ought if it is to be consonant with human nature to be (within limits that are not fixed but variable) a personal appropriation, affirms none the less that the *use* of these goods must be in the common interest (*usus debet fieri communis*) ; and wholly rejects the absolute dominion to which the *jus utendi et abutendi*[1] serves as a pretext.

The Christian world is not the Church. Even in the expression ' the Christian world ' there is a strange ambiguity and in a sense an antinomy. It signifies *Christendom*, the temporal order retained as far as possible by Christian forces within the rule of Justice and of Charity ; and it signifies

[1] In its literal meaning this formula of the Roman Law signifies simply *the right to use and consume* goods. But such a right being affirmed as a divine right, excluding any restriction or limitation or any reference to an end which might regulate the right, property became an idol adapted to a pagan and servile state of society.

the world, from the glamour of which the saints have always averted their thoughts to turn to God. God reigned in the Christian world so far at any rate as one could judge from the essential symbols by which a civilisation recognises its own character. But the devil also had his part in it.

The Church will not perish : the gates of hell shall not prevail against it. The gates of hell have prevailed against the world that was fashioned by the Middle Ages in the West. Under pressure of its own inherent weakness and of open enemies that world has finally gone to pieces before our eyes. We believe that a new Christian order will appear of a wholly different type, of a type which may even now be discernible, or which may be hidden from our view.

ON THE NOTION OF A CONCRETE HISTORICAL IDEAL

Assuming the renaissance of a Christian order in the circumstances of the modern world, what form can one predict that the new Christian order will take ?

Two opposite errors, of a kind familiar to philosophy, must be avoided : one which subjects everything to a univocal interpretation : the other which dissipates everything in equivocal meanings.[1] The

[1] A univocal concept is one which applies in the same way to different things of which it is predicated : thus, the concept of man applies in the same way to Peter and Paul. An 'equivocal term' entirely changes its meaning according as it is applied to one thing and then to another ; thus the term 'balance' used of a pair of scales and of Libia (the Scales), a sign of the Zodiac. On the other hand an 'analogous'

philosophy of the ' equivocal ' school teaches that historical circumstances grow so different with the lapse of time that they come to depend on principles that are also different : as if truth and law and the rules that govern human action were unstable things. A philosopher of the ' univocal ' school will think that these governing rules and principles apply always in the same fashion ; and in particular that the manner in which the Church adjusts its activity to the circumstances of each period and pursues her work in time ought not to vary.

The true solution is to be found in the philosophy of analogy. The notion of order is a notion that is essentially analogous. The principles do not vary ; nor the governing rules of practice : but they are applied in modes that are essentially different and that correspond to one concept only according to a similarity of proportion. And this presupposes that we have something more than an empirical and so to say blind notion of the different phrases of history ; it presupposes that we have a truly rational and philosophic notion of it.

If it is true that in its movement in history civilisation passes under different constellations of dominant signs, we may say that the historical firmament or the historical ideal under which a modern form of Christianity may be imagined is quite different

concept is a concept which is realised in several things in a manner which is purely and simply different and is identical only in a certain measure or relation ; for example, according to a similarity of proportion, in the things of which it is predicated, which accordingly may be diverse in essence though answering to the same idea. Thus the idea of ' knowledge ' is realised in a manner purely and simply different, yet without losing its proper signification, in intellectual and in ' sense ' knowledge.

from the historical firmament or the historical ideal of medieval Christendom.

An attempt to analyse in detail the differences to which we refer would be too long a business to be undertaken here. These differences seem to us to have their centre in a twofold fact : the ideological fact that the ideal or the myth of " realising one's freedom "[1] is the modern substitute for the ideal or the myth of " Force in the service of the Lord " ; and the concrete fact that in the Middle Ages civilisation imperatively demanded unity of religion, whilst to-day it tolerates religious divisions.[2]

We can thus appreciate that the peculiarities and the imperfections of medieval Christianity and those of the new Christianity that is *possible* in modern times are in a sense the inverse one of another.

In following the current of thought one is led to attach a special importance to the idea of the Holy Roman Empire and to the traces it has left in our imagination : for it is plain to see that many of the mental pictures and confused images that subtend our idea of Christianity are unnecessarily controlled by these memories that haunt our imagination. The Holy Roman Empire has in fact been liquidated and dissolved, first by the Treaties of Westphalia, and finally by Napoleon. But it still survives in the imagination as an historical ideal that lies in the past. This ideal too must be sacrificed ; not at all because we think it was in itself an undesirable or an evil thing, but because it has to do with an order that is now at an end.

And here again it is necessary to have recourse

[1] See above, pp. 39 *seqq.*   [2] See above, pp. 62 *seqq.*

to certain philosophical distinctions which alone supply the key to problems in the concrete order. The schoolmen distinguish between an intermediate end (which is a true end though it is subordinated to a higher end) and a means which as such is purely *ad finem* and which is determined by its end.[1] They distinguish again, in the line of efficient causality, between the ' secondary principal cause ' and ' the instrumental cause.'[2] Of these the former, the ' secondary principal cause,' while it is inferior in operation to a secondary cause of a higher order or at any rate to the First Cause, produces none the less an effect proportionate to its specific degree of being. The latter, the instrumental cause, only exerts the causality proper to it in so far as an agent of a higher order lays hold and uses it for the agent's own ends—the instrumental cause thus producing an effect more than proportionate to its specific degree of being.

These distinctions being made, one may observe that in medieval civilisation the things that are Caesar's, though clearly distinguished from the things that are God's, had in some measure a ministerial function towards the latter. To this extent they were an ' instrumental cause ' in relation to the Church ; and their proper end ranked as ' means ' to Eternal Life.

[1] Thus, reasoning is a means to knowing ; the good that one wishes for a loved one is an end—an intermediate end, however, if it does not refer to the Being Who is loved with sovereign love.

[2] Thus the chisel of the sculptor is the instrumental cause of the statue. The sculptor is the principal cause of it, but a secondary principal cause, in subordination to the causality of the architect who designed the building of which the statue is to be an ornament.

In virtue of a process of differentiation in itself natural (though vitiated by false ideologies) the profane or temporal order came in the course of these last centuries to have towards the spiritual order of the Church a relation no longer *ministerial* but autonomous. This altered relation does not necessarily exclude recognition of the primacy of the spiritual order, for there can be subordination between principal agents and between ends ; the subordination of temporal to spiritual being then understood in the sense that the temporal order is a principal agent of lower rank and not an instrumental agent; and the common good of the temporal order being an intermediate end and not a simple means. To this conception rightly understood of the autonomy and subordination of the temporal order belongs the notion of a lay State with a Christian orientation and outlook, which is the only lawful sense that one who accepts the Christian revelation may attribute to the expression ' lay State.' Otherwise, its meaning is either tautologous —and the character of the State signifies only that it is not the Church—or it is vicious and signifies that the State is either ' neutral ' or anti-religious, that is to say, at the service of ends that are purely material or that belong to a counter religion.

If these observations are accurate, it seems that the ideal of a new Christendom will admit two different states or aspects according as it has to do on the one hand with bodies of a wholly lay and temporal character belonging to an economic and political order of a Christian complexion ; or on the other hand with temporal bodies that are simply instruments of the spiritual power.

In the first of these instances the idea of a new Christendom would refer (on the plan of an autonomous temporal order or lay Christian State)[1] to a politico-economic organisation which would guarantee a regular system of co-operation between States, the several members of which would suffer a certain curtailment of sovereignty as the price that has to be paid for the organisation of the international community on a foundation of friendship and of justice.[2]

[1] As is suggested in the foregoing observations, the problem of the ' lay Christian State ' is not without relation to the problem of ' Christian Philosophy ' (see above, p. 70). It would also seem to call for special and searching study, and would doubtless lead to a solution that (*mutatis mutandis*) would be similar.

[2] In handling questions that concern the political community, one must never lose sight of the fact that the social body and the common good are realities that are irreducible to a single enumeration of individuals and of individual goods or virtues. It is not necessary that each citizen who loves his country to the point of being prepared to give his life for it should idealise it in his own special way. It is sufficient that it exists ; it is to its being, formed by a long collective effort through the course of centuries of human history and (though full of imperfections) established by Divine Providence, that his love goes out as it goes out to the being of his parents. For love goes out not to things that are possible but to things that exist. This Being of our fatherland is not the primary Good, it is not the absolute Good, though this is what they mean in practice who deify their country or the State. But it is a real concrete existing good and one which fulfils a special vocation in the great journey of the caravan of human kind : a created good and accordingly not unmixed ; disputed and in peril and on that account more dear. To justify it, there is no need to put forward a false claim to a monopoly of Justice or Liberty or Civilisation or of God Himself—as modern warfare incites governments to do—since to do so is to ask too much of man and disturbs the proper balance between the good of the people and the demands of the State. Here is the tragedy ; and this is the reason why those above all should labour for peace in the world who wish to

In the second instance, the idea of a new Christendom would refer (on the plan of a temporal order as the instrument of the spiritual) to a group of centres of culture and of Christian spirituality spread across the world and receiving their moral (though not their political) unity no longer from a twofold centre, namely the spiritual centre (to wit the Church) and a temporal centre (to wit the Empire) but from the Church alone as sole spiritual centre.

In either view the mental picture that we form gives us an image or concrete ideal which realises in essentially different styles the analogical principle of which the idea of the Holy Roman Empire was an early application.

These reflexions are offered by way of conjecture only but we think it is the business of each one, with the aid of such conjectures, to endeavour to readjust his imagination so that it may be in line with the movement of history.

By virtue of the Charity which is its essential source and principle, Christian spirituality overflows into things outside ; it diffuses its own excellence. It acts upon the world, on culture, on the temporal

---

establish the virtue of patriotism in the hearts of men. An analysis which was free from the vice of nominalism would show that beneath many conceptions of France that inhabit the consciousness of Frenchmen of this or that party there exists not a void nor a simple hope but a lowly and precious human reality, living and abiding, of which every Frenchman (whether he likes it or no) is a member. Pre-eminently of the moral and spiritual order, but incarnate, if this reality escapes definition, it has this in common with things that are individual. It behoves those, however, who have a sense of spiritual things to discern this reality and discover its true features behind the masks in which it is tricked out.

and political order of human life. More than ever in the days to come Christianity will seek to impregnate culture and to save even the temporal life of mankind ; less than ever will it be at peace with the world. But we think the *mode* of its action will be different from what it has been in the past.

It may here be observed that the imagination is by nature ' univocal,' since analogy in the exact sense in which it is used here does not exist in the world of images—and the thoughts of men must often run in the channels of sense or imagination. There follows an inevitable danger, and especially at moments of crisis in history. In our effort to destroy or to defend the invariable yet analogical principles of human order we incline spontaneously to link these principles to a given régime which is perishable, and which it may be is about to perish, and which (it may even happen) has perished long ago.

The spirit of man can escape from this awkward situation only if the Holy Ghost helps him to regain his intelligence. (And the Holy Ghost helps the Church.) In such circumstances one must endeavour to raise one's thought above the level of time, not with a view to the abandonment of the things of time but in order to liberate the mind from ' univocal ' images that hold it in a world of illusion. That is the first step. The next step is to return to the things of time with our thoughts purified and able at once to respect things that are eternal and things that change and (for we are here in the domain of practical life and ethics) out of the flux of movement and of novelty to fashion an order that shall reflect eternal truths in transient things. Those who thought that my *Primauté du Spirituel*[1] was a diary of retreat were gravely mistaken. The aim of that book was to obtain for certain persons a purification of reason and of faith, which should lead to a concentration of these on the one thing necessary, but which might also make them more competent when the time came to impose on material things the primacy that the book was written to affirm.

A DISTINCTION TO BE AVOIDED

In the politico-religious vocabulary of our time no distinction is more fashionable than the distinction between 'thesis' and 'hypothesis.' One often finds behind these words very confused ideas, in which the two errors already referred to[2] are brought into simple juxtaposition for all the world as if one error compensated for the other.

In the statement of the 'thesis' free use is made of univocal concepts in their most summary meaning, whilst with the 'hypothesis' equivocal meanings take their turn. The thesis is stated in a style that is all the more lordly since a secret sense of its ineffectiveness and a secret desire to keep it always always in the realm of theory shield it as far as possible from contact with experience. The hypothesis is all the more abandoned to the easy ways of

[1] English translation: *The Things that are not Caesar's* (Sheed & Ward, 1931).
[2] *Sup.*, p. 103.

opportunism and of liberalism since the present state of the world, of which men have only an empirical awareness, seems entirely remote from a supra-temporal order that is confused with the past as past. Beneath a starry firmament of speculation action is in matters of the purely practical order to all intents and purposes left without principles.

Against this ill-understood notion of thesis and hypothesis we must, I think, set another conception where the distinction is drawn not between a thesis set up in a world cut off from the experience of life and a hypothesis that is the handmaid of opportunism but between what we have called a *concrete historical ideal*, an image that incarnates eternal truth for a given historical firmament and under a form essentially adapted to it, and *the conditions of effective realisation* of this practical ideal. This last is an ideal capable of realisation—with more or less effort, perhaps with extreme difficulty,[1] but there is an essential difference between extreme difficulty and impossibility. In fact, obstacles will appear in the way, the ideal will be realised in a more or less imperfect form, the result may be poor, even nugatory, if you will. The essential point is that the ideal is there, an end capable of being *willed* fully and entirely, and of attracting and giving direction to human energy that will strive more eagerly towards it if the will pursues the ideal in its integrity.

Two separate questions will here occur to the Christian mind. The point has been just now

---

[1] Thus : sanctity is an ideal which is *realisable* by every Christian, according to the condition of each.

formulated, in different terms ; given the age we are now about to enter, what ought the Christian to take for his concrete historical ideal, the dynamic image of the days to come ? The answer needs the collaboration of the philosopher and the man of action. Let us observe that systems of politics, of economics, of sociology only fulfil their office if they descend to the detail of the purely practical order and describe what is to be done here and now for the temporal welfare of mankind : which means, in the field of action, that those who aspire to guide others must be and must be conscious that they are ready (if circumstances permit it) at once to assume power. Before the *coup d'état* of October, 1917, Lenin declared at the Congress of Soviets, and Trotsky notes[1] that it seemed at the time a challenge to good sense, " It is not true that no party is willing at this moment to assume power. There is one party which is bent on doing so. I mean our party." Without entering into a discussion on the nature of the means that were employed, it is in this spirit that, be they Marxist or be they Catholic, men of action should hold themselves in readiness. Otherwise it means that they are afraid of success ; in which case, we ask : why lead an army and invite them to do battle ?

The second question has to do with the limits within which we are able to forecast the effective modes of realisation of this concrete historical ideal. And here it is expedient to bear in mind the dual aspect or state that we have just now distinguished in the ideal of a new Christendom. In

[1] *Lenin* (London, 1925).

the case in which the temporal power is considered as a secondary principal agent or as an intermediate end, the realisation of the Christian ideal is much more difficult than in the case where the temporal power is considered as an instrument or means in the hands of the spiritual power, since in the one case poor temporal means[1] suffice, in the other rich temporal means[2] have to be tried. It is possible none the less that in the actual condition of the world and on the secular basis that we have described, men who were resolved to effect a renewal of the temporal order in conformity with the Christian spirit and by means that were worthy of that spirit would find open before them possibilities much more vast than is ordinarily imagined. And yet it seems that God sets little enough value on the temporal success of his faithful friends and perhaps He desires no more than to offer as a spectacle to our time the complete collapse of visible majesty. In any event it is certain that the action of those who profess the Christian name needs to be radically purged and that men must learn anew not to rely on what to human eyes seems strong nor to be content with appearances. In no department will their action yield results of any value unless it arises from love so pure as to recognise itself as an unprofitable servant and from a will so honest as to seek only the truth.

As to the temporal order considered strictly as means, and the temporal instrument of the spiritual power, it is reasonable to presume that such instruments will be charged in some way with spiritual

[1] See below, p. 133.   [2] See below, p. 133.

114

energies and that they will thus obtain a singular increase in effectiveness, so that they shall appear as so many beacons of fire flashing their light across the whole extent of the earth. In this respect a word used of Pope Pius X in relation to the Lateran Treaty possesses a deep significance : " We seem," he wrote, " to see things brought to the point at which they were realised in the person of St. Francis. He had just enough bodily existence to keep the soul in union with it. . . . The Sovereign Pontiff has now for visible territory just what is indispensable for the exercise of the spiritual authority given to man for the service of mankind. . . . We are content to see the temporal dominion of the Pope restricted within limits so narrow that we can speak of it as taking on a spiritual character by virtue of the vast and sublime and truly divine uses that it is destined to sustain and serve." That is a kind of symbol of the whole temporal order considered as instrument of the spiritual in the way we have been speaking. And in such an order we may fairly maintain an unconditional optimism.

Even if the lay Christian effort failed to renew the visible structure of the world, another task in the temporal order, closely related to the spiritual order, and which indeed takes precedence of the other since it is more close to the proper realm of the spiritual, would always remain for Christendom : the task of infusing into the world almost secretly and from within a certain sap or spirit. Yet must we always suppose that this Christian sap will not be unmixed with blood.

IV

A PARADOX OF HISTORY

One of the paradoxes of history is the connexion which at a certain period of Western culture existed for a time (we have already noticed it) between *bourgeois* society and something which was not religion but which may be called the sociological 'projection' or the sociological 'phenomenon' of religion. The expression 'bourgeois society' or 'capitalist society' which is used in current speech (and which is anyhow inadequate) denotes but one aspect of the world of anthropocentric humanism. And truly the mere idea of any bond or fellowship between Christianity and such a society is itself the height of paradox. The fact that many of our contemporaries are able in good faith to believe that religion and the Church[1] are, as the most telling piece of atheist propaganda puts it, pledged to defend the interests of a class and the

[1] We refer obviously to the Church in its proper and essential being which should be clearly distinguished from the behaviour of these or those of its members in the order of social and temporal affairs. It goes without saying that this distinction has no meaning for those who refuse on principle to recognize any truly spiritual reality and who are thus precluded from seeing in the Church anything save a power in the order of social and temporal affairs. Nor again are our words directed to those who refer every debate in philosophy to a conflict of economic and of class interests and who therefore could conceive only at the cost of a contradiction what is the search for truth. We are inclined to give the maximum of credit to the criticisms that are made of our work ; but it is sheer comedy to allege that St. Thomas Aquinas is a discovery of the rich whose possessions are now in peril and that the determination to find a philosopher who is anti-Marx has led us to consecrate our work to him.

' eminent dignity ' of capitalism and militarism and the rest, is a sign that good faith is not synonymous with intelligence, and that the opinions of men move among shadows where things appear inverted.

The world which issued from the two great revolutions of the Renaissance and the Reformation is in its leading ideas in the spiritual and the cultural sphere downright anti-Catholic. On every occasion on which it has been able freely to follow its instinctive inclination it has persecuted Catholicism ; its philosophy is utilitarian, materialist, or a hypocritical idealism ; its politics are Machiavellian ; its economics liberal and mechanist. The Fathers of bourgeois society are not exactly Fathers of the Church, whether one seeks them with Max Weber in the company of Calvin, or with M. Seillière among the followers of Rousseau ; nor must we omit to mention the Angel of Descartes and his *idées claires*. The modern world sprang out of a great aspiration of the heart of man for the blessing of worldly goods, which is the source of capitalism and mercantilism and industrialism in the economic order, as it is the source of naturalism and rationalism in philosophy. The successive condemnations of usury by the Church stand at the threshold of modern times like a burning interrogatory as to the lawfulness of its economy.

The Church is in the world but is not of the world. If she invites men to be faithful to social institutions that have been tested by time this does not mean that she is tied to one or other of these institutions ; it signifies her recognition that the stability of law is an important element in the welfare of mankind.

The Church has constantly shewn in the course of history that political and social changes have no terrors for her and that she has a sense singularly free from illusion of the contingent character of human institutions. She teaches obedience to temporal authority and to just laws since all legitimate rule of man over man comes from God ; but (saving the case of a temporal power having a ministerial rule in regard to the spiritual authority, as happened with the Empire in the Middle Ages) the Church does not institute the temporal authority, she sanctions the rule of him who is in office— without forbidding efforts to effect a change of government, and without forbidding resistance, by force if need be, to tyrannical rule. With a view to the advancement of her work for the salvation of souls, and so that States also shall respect the ends that are proper to the spiritual nature of man, the Church seeks to act in harmony with the secular power. But she is not unaware that at most times— since the world which turns away from God is subject to a Prince who is not God (*totus in maligno positus est mundus*)—to deal with the temporal power is a little like dealing with the devil. And on the whole one devil is as good as another. A new ruler who establishes his authority cancels out the rights of his predecessor. In truth the Catholic Church took a long time to adjust itself to the bourgeois régime, perhaps because the medieval order which was framed under her protection continued to occupy a place in her memory as it had so long occupied her guardian care. M. Groethuysen has gone so far as to write a book in which he makes this slow adjustment a matter of reproach. The Church has never been tied to the existing régime, and to whatsoever persecutions she may be exposed in those régimes that follow (she is used to persecutions —*supra dorsum meum fabricaverunt peccatores*[1]) we may well believe she will not regret its passing. She has no bond with it.

BANKRUPTCY OF A WORLD IN APPEARANCE CHRISTIAN

To understand the paradox of which we have just been speaking and the way in which men came to believe that religion was tied by its principles to ' bourgeois ' or ' capitalist ' society, we must penetrate into a world of appearance and of confusion. This illusory belief has its origin in the fundamental confusion (to which attention has already been drawn[2]) between the *Church* and the *Christian world ;* or between the Catholic religion and the social behaviour of the common run of the Catholics of the ruling classes—in short between the spiritual and the temporal orders. The Church as such has the promise of eternal life, and the Prince of this world has no part with her. He has his place, as we have said, in the Christian world.

The Christian world which issued from the dissolution of medieval Christendom condoned many iniquities—I refer here to a sort of collective failure in the course of history, for which it is senseless to seek to attach responsibility to individuals.

Etenim non potuerunt mihi.   [2] See page 102.

This is the world which God is allowing to sink under its burden of death, while new life is forming in the womb of time.

The mission of such a one as Léon Bloy was to herald these things and to cry them from the roof tops. It is strange to observe to what a degree an avowal of this kind seems indecent to many Christians even to-day. They seem to be apprehensive lest they should embarrass apologetic. They judge it better to lay the blame on the craft of wicked men and to treat history after the manner of the Manicheans, arguing as if wicked men were not subject to the government of God but only to that of the devil. The Jews of old and even the Ninevites did not stand on so much ceremony.

The failure of which we speak is that of the social or cultural mass taken in its (imperfect) unity, in its corporate institutions and its ' objective ' spirit rather than as a series of individuals taken one by one, and thus it refers primarily to the social order or rather to the spiritual order incarnate in it. It is, we may say, the failure of the civilisation that is called Christian and of each of us to the extent to which we are identified with that civilisation.

" Those to blame are the Christians themselves ; the old Christian world ; not the Christian religion to be sure, but its adepts who very often have shown themselves to be poor Christians. The gospel which, instead of being translated into terms of life, passes into a conventional form of rhetoric and takes shelter behind actual evil and real injustice, that gospel cannot but arouse revolt against it. . . . The posture of Christian society in face of communism is not only the posture of one who carries in his heart eternal and absolute truth ; it is also the posture of the culprit who had failed to live this truth ; who has betrayed it."[1] Nicholas Berdyaev, whose metaphysics are to us unacceptable but whose views on human life and history are often profound, here speaks capital truths that cannot be disputed. We prefer to try and fathom the reasons for this fact of history.

A first reason is general in character. It springs from the universal truth that evil is more common than good among men. It is therefore natural that there should be more ' bad Christians ' than ' good Christians ' in a Christian society and especially in the higher (and therefore more exposed) strata of that society. From the moment when such a society loses its essential spirit and the institutions that were linked to it (as happened to Christendom from the onset of the Renaissance and the Reformation) a new collective consciousness arises whose spirit grows more heavy and sombre the more it deviates from the vital centre of the faith and of the Church. And thus one reaches the ' naturalisation ' of religion of which we have written elsewhere,[2] and the exploitation of Christianity by deist or atheist (there is no practical difference) for temporal ends. The thesis that religion is ' good for the people ' had developed mightily in the period of enlightened despotism and seems to have been given a political direction (and to

---

[1] Nicholas Berdyaev : *Problème du Communisme : Questions disputées.*
[2] Cf. *Religion and Culture*, p. 58 *et seq.*

have been turned to the advantage of the Prince) before it was given an economic direction (and turned to the advantage of the Rich). " This cult of the marvellous seems positively made for the people," wrote Frederick the Second ; and again, " I cannot imagine anyone exercising his mind about the question : is it lawful to deceive the people ? I am going to see that it is done." The Academy of Berlin put the question up to competition in 1780. " To this question," replied Johann Freidrich Gillet, one of the prizemen in the competition : " Yes, in my opinion it may be done if weighty and sufficient reasons exist. The people are merely folk. They will ever so remain and ought so to remain. And besides, the history of every age and of our own proves by a multitude of instances that the deception of the people has always brought much benefit to the people and to their leaders."

The weakness of human nature thus affords a simple and natural explanation why so many Christians, lay and ecclesiastic, went so far to excuse and honour and flatter the owners of moneybags in a period when the possession of money was coming to be the principal source of power in society, just as there are those who are ready to pay their respect to military or popular power or power of any other species when it becomes predominant. These truths are too current to merit more detailed examination.

But of the historical failure of which we are speaking there are causes of a more special kind that have a closer relation to the problem under examination. We shall attempt, however imperfectly, to indicate these causes.

In medieval Christendom, civilisation, living so to say *in utero Ecclesiae*, sought under the spontaneous impulse of the Faith and almost without reflecting to translate the precepts of the Gospel not only in the spiritual life of citizens but also in the institutions of the temporal and the social order. When with the ' reflective age ' the inner differentiation of culture became a leading feature of life, and art and science and philosophy and the State began each to be conscious (with what an awful conscience) of itself, it is perhaps not inaccurate to say that there was no similar study of the social order as such or of the essential nature of its being. How indeed could such a study happen in a world which was to grow to greatness under the ascendancy of Descartes ?

Through the voluntary and most praiseworthy manifestations of corporal and spiritual mercy the Christian spirit of love sought in the course of these last centuries to remedy the injustice and the shortcomings of the social order. It may fairly be said nevertheless that there was wanting an *instrument* of the philosophical and cultural order, an awareness, a discernment of the essential character of the temporal order and of the life of man on earth, which would enable the Christian mind in opposition to the intellectual currents of the time (for it was the period of the dissolution of Christian ideas) to assess in the order of speculative and of practical knowledge the value of the institutions of economic and social life from the point of view of the realisation of the Gospel precepts in the social and temporal order. During this period the spirit of the Gospels was not

123

wanting to the living and saintly members of the Christian world, but there was wanting an explicit and proper awareness of one of the areas of life in which this Spirit was to be applied. And though the claim of Auguste Comte to be the inventor of social science may be largely inadmissible, it may fairly be argued that the ' scientific ' illusions of sociology—and likewise of socialism—have assisted the children of light by obliging them to explore with the aid of philosophic reflection these areas of human life and activity.

These reflexions make it evident that, from the point of view of the social possibilities of Christianity and of the full appreciation of the demands of the Gospel precepts in relation to the temporal institutions of the State, the culture of Christian peoples is even now in an extremely backward condition. They also help us to see how it happened that good and pious souls who practise the maxims of Christianity in their private lives and in their individual relations with others seem suddenly, as soon as they encounter the special order of relations and the moral system *sui generis* that appertain to social life as such[1] to pass to a different plane and to follow the principles of naturalism. And finally these reflexions help us to understand how the change which by slow degrees displaced the economic régime of the Middle Ages and substituted the régime of moneylending and of capitalism (though from the beginning it raised among Christian

---

[1] One recalls the scandalized attitude of certain Catholic employers (otherwise excellent men) in face of the Encyclical *Rerum Novarum*.

folk many questions that touch the conscience of individuals and the confessional) was not for such a length of time appreciated and adjudged by the Christian mind (which had in truth been educated on Cartesian lines) from the point of view of its social significance and worth. And so the capitalist régime became established throughout the world, with passive resistance and secret hostility on the part of Catholic social bodies, but without provoking any active, deliberate or effective opposition from Christian folk or from organised Christian or even Catholic communities.

One ought however to observe that the Catholic conscience did not fail to make its protest heard. In the nineteenth century in particular, at the very time when Capitalism was about to reach maturity and was taking possession of the world, men like Ozanam and Vogelsang and La Tour de Pin raised up their voices. And above all the Church itself made good the shortcomings of Christian society by formulating the principles and the essential truths that govern the whole field of economic affairs and that the established order of modern societies largely fails to recognise. The formulation of these truths and principles is to be found in the doctrinal declarations of Pope Leo XIII on the social order and in the encyclicals of Pope Pius XI that echo these declarations. It is indisputable that these interventions of the Popes and the Catholic activities that they have stimulated and directed have already had a profound effect on legislation and on public opinion.

THE TEMPORAL MISSION OF CHRISTIAN FOLK

We are witnesses at the present moment of an event in history of outstanding importance, of an event that we may call the Christian *Diaspora*. I mean that the family or society of Christians scattered among the peoples of the earth, or, if you will have it so, the Christian laity, have begun to develop at once an explicit reflective and deliberate consciousness of its true cultural mission and of the true nature of the social body considered as a social whole. And at a moment when the Church, having come through the crises of the nineteenth century in which she had to fight for life and liberty, is in the act of resuming the leadership of the intellectual life of Christendom, this Christian consciousness is developing and is in our view likely to develop more and more a sense of hostility to capitalist materialism as well as to communist materialism which is merely its consequence. One who bears in mind the laboured and discordant efforts of religious thought in the nineteenth century, and the embarrassment it suffered through lack of light on the loftier planes of philosophy and theology and the splendid truths that it was yet able to proclaim, is led to believe that one of the tasks to the achievement of which our age is called is the reconciliation of the vision of Joseph de Maistre and that of Lamennais in the higher unity of the supreme wisdom of which St. Thomas Aquinas is the herald to our time.

It is not in the name of the materialist conception of history or in virtue of Marxist theories like the

126

theory of surplus values or by rejecting in principle
the institution of private property that capitalist
economics should be criticised. Such criticism
should be made rather in the name of ethical and
spiritual values and of the primary social value of
human personality, holding fast to the principle that
the rational life of man is ordered to the accomplishment of true freedom of autonomy. From this
point of view, though the type of economy which lies
at the base of the capitalist régime is not in abstract
principle or in its ideal scheme fundamentally
immoral, as Marx thought, it must none the less
be confessed, as we have tried to show elsewhere,
that in point of fact, and tested not only by its ideal
operation but also by the spirit it has shown in
history and by the actual ways in which this spirit
has become manifest in the institutions of human
society, the capitalist régime is wedded to the
unnatural principle of the fertility of money.
" Instead of being considered as a mere feeder
enabling a living organism, which the productive
undertaking is, to procure the necessary material,
equipment, and replenishing, money has come to
be considered *the living organism* and the undertaking with its human activities as the feeder and
instrument of money ; so that the profits cease to be
the normal fruit of the undertaking fed with money,
and become the normal fruit of the money fed by the
undertaking. Values have been reversed and the
immediate consequence is to give the rights of
dividend precedence over those of wages and salary
and to establish the whole economy under the
supreme regulation of the laws and the fluidity

127

of the *sign* money predominating over the *thing*, commodities useful to mankind."[1]

To criticise such an economic system the Christian makes appeal to the holy name of Justice, a daughter of the Lord, of which the idea is excluded from every materialist system and of which the power is covertly used by materialist revolutionaries though they dare not avow it even in their secret heart. The Christian is not compelled by his system of thought to dissemble the idea of justice as a thing of which he is ashamed. He is free to set it forth in the full light of day. Justice is strong; it leads a long way.

Granted a sane theory of values, of work and of ownership, the mechanism of the contract of partnership or co-operation affords a justification in law and equity for the profits that accrue to invested capital and in this sense we have just pointed out that the capitalist economy is accredited to an ideal type which is not objectionable or sinful in itself.[2] But in the order of concrete reality it is a vicious economy[3] ; in actual fact this contract of partnership

[1] *Religion and Culture.* English translation (Sheed & Ward, 1931), p. 62.

[2] Cf. *Summa theol.*, ii-ii, 78, 2, ad. 5.

[3] In the medieval scholasticism, as Sombart has observed, " a clear distinction was drawn between the investment of capital and lending money at interest, two operations that are opposed even in principle (cf. *Summa theol.*, loc. cit.). But in proportion as money, especially since the 15th century, became mistress of the instruments of production, capital *as a thing*, an instrument and means of production, was destined, in that collective estimation which is so to say the formative idea of an economic régime, to be comprehended in money, and at the same time the idea of the fertility of money began to take root ; in such wise that the two operations of an opposing kind of which Sombart speaks tended to merge and be confused. It is this process (in conjunction with the nominalist decline of medieval thought, and with the dislocation of values that appears in Puritanism and the enthronement of material

operates as a moneylending contract and usury makes its appearance as the sovereign mistress of the bourgeois world. How could it fail to *use* man to the bone? The energies that foster and maintain its life are increasingly undermined by a deadly sin, not indeed a sin which kills the souls of individuals who are forced to live in the midst of this world and to use its mechanism, but a sin which brings death in time to the social body : the cult of earthly riches coming to form the soul of its civilisation. The spirit of Capitalism considered objectively is a spirit of exaltation of active and inventive power, of the dynamic energies of man and of individual enterprise ; but it is a spirit of hatred of poverty and of contempt of the poor. The poor man is there as an instrument, not as a human personality ; and if after abandoning him, in the very days that followed on the declaration of the Rights of Man, to be oppressed and degraded and reduced to the limit of human endurance, a movement was later started to raise and improve his condition, this movement sprang from the realisation that the instrument might otherwise become dangerous and also that it gives better results when it is clean and in good order, even in good moral order.[1] In his turn again, the rich

---

prosperity as a sign of salvation, and other like elements) that gave birth to the capitalist system of economy, which after a long period of incubation was established in history only in the second half of the 18th century and is distinguished not only by the importance it attached to the function of capital but also (and it is really a separate matter) by the perversion of this function in the direction of usury.

[1] [For a grim illustration, see a letter to the *Times* newspaper, dated 23 October, 1934, under the heading *Welfare of the Worker*. Tr.]

man exists only as consumer or paunch, not as a human personality; and the tragedy of such a civilisation is that to maintain and develop the monstrous economy of Usury or Moneylending, it is necessary to aim at making all men consumers or rich; but then if there are no more poor men to act as instruments the whole economy comes to an end and perishes. And it perishes also, as we have seen in our day, if there are not enough consumers to set the instruments to work.

The objective spirit of Capitalism is a spirit of bold and courageous conquest of the earth; but it is a spirit of the enslavement of all things to the endless increase of the sacred pile of material goods.[1]

[1] Cf. the classical analysis of Sombart in his book *Le Bourgeois*. Haesslé has summarized his analysis. " The capitalist draws no personal good from his fortune save only the irrational sense of success in business. It is just this sterile asceticism which appears incomprehensible and mysterious, base and contemptible to the eyes of the man of pre-capitalist civilization for whom only a perversion of mind, the *auri sacra fames*, can explain why men should sacrifice their life solely to go to their grave laden with material wealth. ' When with Puritanism the Capitalist spirit and asceticism invaded England, this asceticism was like a belt of fire round the body of merry England. . . . It prescribed a levelling of morals, a system of standardization, that excluded as valueless everything that was not of immediate utility in the economic order.' At the touch of Capitalism everything fades, all moral and spiritual values die. There remains only Chaos. One's homeland becomes a strange country; nature, art, literature, the State, friendship, all are lost in a mysterious Nothingness for the man ' who has no time.' Modern Capitalism,' says Max Weber, ' leads to the mechanization of all life, external and even internal.' At first sight it seems surprising that Sombart should divide mankind into two categories, ' erotics ' and ' bourgeois,' and that he should range the Capitalist in the second category which consists of those who have lost Love. But may not this theory of Sombart contain a profound truth ? And is not the total absence of Love (in the Christian sense) at the root of all the social evils of our time ? " Johannès Haesslé, *Le Travail*, pp. 345–346.— On the present condition of Capitalism, cf. Werner Sombart, *L'Apogée du Capitalisme* (Payot, Paris, 1932).

Like all things in history it has elements of good and evil, of light and darkness, but it is its dark countenance that is now offered to the world. *Jam judicatus est*. Truth to tell, the Christian conscience has now only to take cognisance of this judgment. Let the dead body, the corpse of four centuries of labour and pain, of beauty, of heroism, and of crime, be buried by other dead, with speeches and conferences and wars and fireworks or red flags. The Christian is not without a sense of the sadness of this spectacle of death, but his face is set towards life.

And yet has not this awareness of which we have spoken come too late ? If Christian thought gathers its treasures of speculative and practical wisdom into a bouquet (so to say) of free and authoritative statement, is it to offer its gift to hands that are already in the decay of death ; to a world that has lost the power to take and hold it ? Is it the object of all its effort to comfort itself with the mere thought of what might have been ?

It may be that the reckoning against the existing order is too heavy and that it is doomed to an evil end. But the end of *a* world is not the end of *the* world. We know not the age for which we labour. If it were true that a Christian renaissance would now come *too late* to save the world that is heir to Luther and Descartes and Rousseau it would by the same token come *too soon* in relation to a new age of culture. There will be other days to come after the dissolution of the world of that inheritance ; and new beginnings to be made. But the truth is that human freedom plays a greater and more mysterious part in history than men are apt to think. In a sense everything depends on man. If his spirit is free, events follow from his free decision. Finally, even supposing that the Christian effort should fail to reform the existing world in the secular order as such or in the temporal order considered as an (intermediate) end, we are convinced it will not fail, no matter what the opposition may be, in the temporal order considered as a means or instrument of the spiritual, in the Christendom of the spiritual order that has " just enough body to keep the soul in union with it " ; and that will always elude the material forces that may be used against it. *Transiens per medium illorum, ibat.*

We have seen above why a distinction must be made between these two orders or cases. It would be absurd to seek to sacrifice one to the other ; our effort must be directed against both at once. But in accordance with the essential hierarchy of values it must be admitted that the order of " poor temporal means " takes precedence of the order of " rich temporal means,"[1] even as the spiritual order takes precedence of the whole temporal order. To fail to recognise this subordination is to offend against that which one claims to defend, and to aggravate the evil. The transformation for which we must hope involves a much more radical revolution than that which is envisaged by the writings of the revolutionaries : for the communist revolution is a crisis through which the tragedy of a civilisation that has for its highest ideal the enjoyment of terrestrial goods and the primacy of matter reaches its logical *dénouement*. The radical principles of

[1] See page 133, *infra* and note thereto.

capitalist disorder are not altered but only accentuated. For the Christian on the other hand the work
of reform involves the changing of those radical
principles and of the whole orientation of our cultural
life. In a word, the common object of our effort is
the transfiguration of the world. And to the extent
to which something of the kind may happen in
history, it is clear that God will be the *principal
agent ;* and men, whether they resist or assist, mere
instruments.

The problem which at this point forces itself on
our attention if we wish to be instruments in the
style of sons and not of slaves is that of the Purification of Means. We must distinguish three incom-
mensurable orders of Means, of which each has its
proper law : rich temporal means ; poor temporal
means ; and spiritual means ; or, following a slightly
different mode of division,[1] which will be the subject
of the next chapter, material means ; spiritual
means directed to the temporal order ; purely
spiritual means. Each of these orders is subject
in its turn to the rule of Christian ethics ; and the
hierarchy that exists between the orders is inviolable.
All things have their origin in the spiritual order ;
the transformations in the temporal order have their
beginnings in the supra-temporal. On the history
even of the world and of civilisation falls the sentence
of St. John of the Cross : " Love is the principle
by which ye shall be judged."

[1] The first mode of division is based rather on the relation
between the means used and the force that is necessary to put
them into operation ; the second mode on the nature of the
means in their own essential character. The sling of David
was a poor means in relation to the spiritual force that used it ;
and was in its essential character a material or temporal means.

THE EXTENT OF NECESSARY CHANGE

We have just used the word revolution. We may be permitted to draw attention to the difference that exists between the use of a common noun (*a* revolution or revolutions) and the use of a personal or proper noun (*the* revolution). In this second case the word revolution is charged with a definite historical meaning and is part of the inheritance of a certain body of men, of those who have sought most ardently to establish the reign of anthropocentric humanism : the communists are their most typical representatives at the present time. And the mere circumstance that the thing it designates has been thus personified naturally tends to make of ' the revolution ' or ' the revolutionary spirit ' the supreme standard of values and of action : it is plain (as was pointed out in one of the answers submitted to the inquiry instituted in December, 1932, by the Nouvelle Revue Francaise) that willy-nilly in these circumstances men accept the leadership of those who at the moment represent the pure type of the revolutionary spirit taken as the supreme test of values.

That the world has entered on a revolutionary period is now a matter not of controversy but of record. One is accordingly entitled to declare oneself a revolutionary in order to mark one's intention to rise to the height of the occasion and one's understanding of the necessity for radical reform that will change in their distinctive ' humanist-inhuman ' character the essential principles of our existing régime of civilisation.

But the deepest and most efficacious of these principles lie in the spiritual order. And the term ' revolution ' signifies through the imagery with which it is associated in the mind large changes of the visible order. If these associated images were to divert thought and desire to visible and tangible things, to the external and sensible and quick (and easy) things as the things of most importance, and if they led men to believe in the primary value of immediate results and of 'rich temporal means '[1] it would involve a deep deception. The first supporters of the October Revolution in Russia were intellectuals who desiring a spiritual revolution mistook for a reform born of spiritual principles an upheaval in the visible and sensible order that masked the crisis of the old illness that afflicts the modern mind. Lenin got rid of them by expeditious means after they had served his turn.

Péguy used to say that the social revolution will be a moral revolution or it will not be at all. To wish to change the face of the earth without first changing one's heart (which no man can do of his own strength) is to undertake a work that is purely destructive. Perhaps indeed if omnipotent love did truly transform our hearts, the exterior work of reform would already be half done.

All this shows, it would seem, that it is better to be revolutionary than to call oneself a revolutionary and especially at a time when the Revolution has become the most conventional of commonplaces and a title that is claimed by men of every kind.

[1] See p. 133

To disown this name might conceivably be a useful act of ' revolutionary courage.'

In any case " the rupture between the Christian order and the established disorder " has to do *not only* with things in the economic or the political order but with the whole range of culture, with the relation of the spiritual and the temporal orders, and even with the conception we ought to have of the work of man here below and at this moment in the history of the world. It has to do *not only* with the external and visible order of human life; it has to do *also and primarily* with its spiritual bases. The rupture will become manifest in external things, in the visible and tangible order. But it is an ineluctable condition that it should fulfil itself first in the intellect and heart of those who wish to be co-workers with God in history ; and that they should appreciate it in its proper fulness and depth of meaning.

ON THE PURIFICATION
OF THE MEANS

ON THE PURIFICATION OF MEANS

THE POSSIBILITY OF A RECONSTRUCTION OF THE TEMPORAL ORDER ON CHRISTIAN PRINCIPLES

1. Many efforts at social reform run the risk (which we pointed out on a previous page) of underestimating the extent of the transformation at which they aim when they seek to infuse the spirit of authentic humanism—the spirit of the Gospel—into the temporal or cultural order. For this transformation involves changes both in the internal and in the external régime of human life, changes that must be effected in the heart of man and in the body politic ; changes that have to do, though in different ways, with the visible social order and with the invisible moral and spiritual order ; and primarily with the spiritual order, for of its own right the spiritual order takes rank before the social order. The disadvantage of the word 'revolution' and of the imagery that it evokes is not that it makes men aspire to changes that are too radical or too extensive but on the contrary that the change it contemplates is based on derivative principles only and that its magnitude is confined to the order of sensible appearances ; to a great and sudden upheaval whose reforming energy in the material and external order masks its lack of essential and spiritual depth ; a change which is in truth a mere

139

rearrangement of things within the material order. The world is looking for reform which is more (to borrow a phrase of Lucien Bonaparte) than " the turning over of a dung-hill."

2. That fundamental changes in our existing civilisation are inevitable ; that the age in which we live is a revolutionary age ; that the outline of the structure and certain of the general characteristics of the new world are already in a state of formation ; these are things that spring from those ' necessities of history ' which are the outcome of a multitude of free acts done over the course of centuries and years now past and bearing their effect in time. Before these necessities the wills of the men of the present day are powerless ; impotent to affect the existence of what may be called the generic demand for radical change which marks our time, and which yet remains in certain essentials undefined and undetermined. The will of man is obliged also to recognise this other fact : that the logic of historical failure and the inclination of our human weakness to follow the line of least resistance importunately urge this undefined demand for radical change to seek fulfilment in easy courses and inferior ways. The question arises whether there are not other modes of fulfilment, born of the forces of rectification and of revival which are also inherent in human history, that will give *their* character and direction to these tendencies and this demand. And that depends on the wills of men of our time : on the presence and the action of a few men, of a few heroic souls, if such there be, of a few men (if

there are any such) with a touch of genius in the field of action.

If such men are to be found within the Christian field, then, however improbable existing difficulties may make it appear, a renewal of the world on Christian principles may possibly be effected : though it will carry all the marks of imperfection and of precariousness that go with every human achievement. The mere possibility of success makes it reasonable for men of action to take such a reform as their goal in the temporal order. And even if their effort fails, it will not wholly fail ; for their witness at least will live.

On principle the task requires that human wills shall exert all their energies to carry the work to a successful issue, and that they shall at the same time maintain a certain detachment even against the event of their success : a detachment arising not from indifference but from magnanimity ; not from defect but from excess of love ; a detachment that involves no lack of interest.

The spirit of detachment does not impair, it even perfects, the devotion and the effectiveness of their effort. For men of action to preserve a spirit of detachment in face of visible success is a great cross ; but to work for a renewal of the temporal order on Christian principles yet not to work in a truly Christian spirit would be to spoil the thing that exists in an effort to bring it into being : which is the most subtle form of treason.

Those who attempt to bring a Christian spirit of order into this material world must accordingly be on their guard from the beginning against the temptation that is offered by visible success. For that matter, if revolutions commonly lose their sincerity of principle from the moment of their success, it is really only by virtue of such sincerity that they do succeed. " The greatest strength lies with the single-minded " : this saying of Zola gives the efficient principle of every great reform in history. It is necessary only that those who seek to establish a régime of Christian order in the world should ponder the awful implications of the principle in their own case. The single-mindedness of a St. Just or a Lenin is rare enough in their own order ; and that is relatively simple by comparison to the single-mindedness which is required of Christian reformers : and of which they know the name.

" THE SOCIAL REVOLUTION WILL BE A MORAL REVOLUTION OR NOT AT ALL "

3. This saying is open to misinterpretation. It does not mean that before a reform of the social order can be made effective all men must first be converted to virtuous living. Interpreted in this way, the saying would be merely a pharisaical pretext for avoiding any effort at social reform. Revolutions are the work of comparatively small groups of men who devote all their energy to the task : it is to these men that the words of Péguy are addressed. His meaning is : You can only transform the social order of the modern world by effecting at the same time and first of all within

your own soul a renewal of moral and spiritual life : by digging down to the moral and spiritual foundations of human existence, and reviving the moral ideas that govern the life of the social body as such ; and by awakening a new impulse in the secret sources of its being.

The Russian communists have clearly appreciated these truths : they have even formed their party into a kind of brotherhood with an exacting and rigorous discipline, and by every means in their power they endeavour to renew after their fashion the moral bases of life of the whole people, so that what gives their materialist and atheist revolution its deepest power of attracting the souls of men (concurrently even with the satisfaction of the old appetite of pride and violence and with the exaltation of the splendour of display) is the indestructible spiritual appeal (unconfessed because it is not in accordance with the Marxian table of values) of Justice and Poverty, of Fortitude in suffering. For Justice in an illusory form, and Poverty and Fortitude endured but not savoured, crown with a mirage of divine virtues the Monastery of the Godless that is Soviet Russia.

Looked from the point of view of the mystical interpretation of history, it would seem that the Soviet war against God, with its apparatus of lies and nonsense, is the symbol of divine wrath which tolerates the blasphemy of pure negation in order to put an end to the blasphemy of an affirmation which had come to be falsehood on the lips of so many soi-disant Christians in whose heart a strange mixture of ' Holy Russia ' and the profanation of

143

the Divine Names had reached the last stages of decay. Who knows whether fresh and authentic flowers of the human spirit may not shoot forth again from the essential root of human nature now prepared and cleansed by the spiritual scourge of militant atheism that stalks the earth ? Meantime, we know that the general line of dialectic materialism which has been traced by the philosophers of the Soviet State postulates the reintegration in Matter of liberty, spontaneity, and psychical and other elements that are recognised as indispensable to the dynamism of the proletarian movement and to the development of revolutionary power, and to a spiritual impetus that it is desired not to destroy but to domesticate. The congenital weakness (whatever be the possible merits of its executants) of this State philosophy which has no integrity in the speculative order and which causes the very notion of truth to perish in the soul, does not save it from avowing under compulsion and in its own odd way (wrapping them in the garment of a pseudo-scientific hylozoism) the essential importance in history of the forces of freedom ; thus demon-strating to what an extent every effective work of social reform depends on the existence of an heroic ideal. In this matter the lesson of old Sorel has been learned alike by Communism and by Fascism.

4. But has the true and perfect heroism, the heroism of love, no lesson to offer ? Once the Christian conscience comes to realise the essential character of social life, with its distinctive being and reality and technique, will not Christian sanctity

have to enter and labour in the same field in which the Hammer and Sickle and the Fasces and the Swastika are severally pursuing their heroic task ? Is it not high time that sanctity should descend from the heaven of cloistered life that four centuries of the Baroque spirit had reserved for it, descend to the world of secular culture and labour in social and political affairs with a view to the reform of the temporal order of mankind ? Yes, indeed; on condition that it retains its sanctity and does not lose its character on the way. There is the rub.

The Christian body has at such a time as ours two opposite dangers that it needs to avoid : the danger of seeking sanctity only in the desert, and the danger of forgetting the need of the desert for sanctity ; the danger of enclosing in the cloister of the interior life and of private virtue the heroism it ought to share among mankind, and the danger of conceiving this heroism, when it overflows into social life and endeavours to transform it, in the same manner as its materialist opponents : according to a purely external standard ; which is to pervert and dissipate it. Christian heroism has not the same sources as heroism of other kinds. It has its source in the heart of a God scourged and turned to scorn and crucified outside the city gate.

It is time for Christian sanctity again as in the centuries of the Middle Age to put its hand to the things of earth but with the consciousness that its strength and majesty are from elsewhere and of another order. It is possible that before the end a day will come on which it will meet again in the City of Time with Glory and Triumph of a visible

145

order. For the time being it is manifest (and a stumbling block to many) that visible majesty and the tumult and the shouting of glorious emprise are on the side of the enemy : majesty of an imperfect kind, but majesty as the flesh and the world define it. The Five Years' Plan and the March on Rome are surely worthy of the Statue of Nabuchodonosor.

The Church does not now lead Empires to Canossa. She concentrates her mighty power in a struggle that is at once hard and obscure, on the humble duty of the salvation of souls. To keep men from doing too serious hurt to their spiritual welfare, She has to have dealings with Powers whose hands are doubtfully clean or even unclean, and who rage against the spirit of Jesus. They are blind who attack her on this score, being ignorant of times and seasons. The hour at which Christ is nailed to the Cross is not a convenient time at which to ask Him to change water into wine or to multiply loaves and fishes. In that hour something is being enacted that is greater than miracles. The Resurrection will take place ; but after the expiration of three days.

If only He will come down from the Cross, that we may see and believe : *ut videamus et credamus.* If only the Church will leave the Cross and ravish our eyes with her beauty and majesty, then shall we believe in her God. Foolish they who reverse the order of things and make the Faith vain by wishing to see before believing ; they range themselves on the side of woe. For they have been declared blessed who believe before they see and that they may see : *Beati qui non viderunt et crediderunt.*

146

Has our time any chance of witnessing a transformation of the temporal order on Christian principles ? In any event such a transformation cannot be expected to be achieved in the same way and by the same means as other reforms and revolutions of the temporal order. It is in its essence a function of Christian heroism. A renewal of the social order on Christian lines will be a work of Sanctity or it will not occur at all.

5. This reflection, as we have seen above, has significance chiefly for the relatively limited number of those by whose efforts such a reform might be effected. But of whom are we to think in this connexion ? Of what body having existence in history ? Here is a new problem.

It is fairly clear that reform and revolution of the temporal régime are not the affair of the Church, which has not a temporal but an eternal and a spiritual end above and beyond political and social issues. The Church takes particular care not to become an adherent of any particular régime or class or party.

For the same reason reform and revolution of the temporal order are not the affair of what is called in our day Catholic Action. For Catholic action is the concern of the Church. It is the work of the lay apostolate acting under the direction of the hierarchy. The pressure of events in the course of these last years has led Catholics to take more careful note of its definition and its nature. Essentially an affair of the Church, Catholic action is referable to the spiritual order or the spiritual sword; its formal cause or character is purely spiritual. Not that Catholic action should ignore or take no interest in the temporal order : far from it. But when it makes contact with the things of the temporal order—social, economic, political—it does so from the point of view of the spiritual values they are involved and govern that order. By a kind abstraction that is made necessary by the hierarchies and complexities of nature, Catholic action contemplates in the temporal order the spiritual values on which that order depends and which are invested in it; the Christian spirit, Christian principles, Christian truths of the specula- tive and the practical order which ought to inform it. It does not contemplate the temporal as such, and stands aloof from the specific life of the temporal order, being as little interested as the Church itself in the strife of parties.

Nevertheless Catholics are not cut off from time or separated by their faith from the things of this world, from civilisation and from the State. Instead, their Faith makes them more sensitive to their duties as creatures assigned to a particular con- juncture of space and time and entangled in the web of worldly events. It bids them there also to serve their Master, who is King of Time as He is of Eternity, of Civilisations as He is of Souls. How then and in what right shall they work directly for the proper good of the temporal State ? Clearly, in right of their citizenship of their particular State, as citizens having such and such convictions, such and such an ideal and above all such and such a religion, such and such a conception of God and of the world—not in right of their membership of the Church or as citizens of the Eternal City.

Shall they then constitute within the State a Catholic Party, a political body Catholic in character and in name ? The passing " unwept and un-honoured " of the German Centre Party is sufficient to show to those who had not already realised it the essential drawback of such a hybrid conception, which belongs to a past century. A *Catholic Political Party* ordained by its very constitution (as a *political* party) to temporal things and differentiated by religion (as a *Catholic* party) runs a twofold risk ; in the first place of compromising the welfare of Catholicism and of individual souls in the affairs of the world, of degrading the things of the spirit and of reducing them to the level of the temporal and of the particular ; of confounding religion with politics and the conduct of a particular party ; and in the second place of failing at certain times in the duty it owes to the temporal interests it is formed to serve, by hesitating to involve the glory of a great name in risks and enterprises of a purely terrestrial order which are often (even to the point of hazard) essential for the protection of those interests.

To what conclusion then do we inevitably come, if not to the conception of political bodies distin-guished by their political or temporal character, no matter to what extent they may be guided by religious influences ? A political party of such and such a political denomination formed and directed by Catholics is a very different thing from a Catholic political party. Even though the in-spiration of active faith be stronger in it, and though

149

the primacy of the spiritual order be more effectively recognised, politics are not compromised with clericalism, nor religion with politics. I have said a party, one ought to say parties, for there is obviously no reason why Catholics should be concentrated in one political party. Taken separately indeed the interests of Catholicism (*secundum hominem dico*) would seem to be not that all Catholics should be grouped as far as possible in a single party (however powerful it might appear) but rather that there should be a majority of Catholics in all the decent political parties—assuming always that modern States will continue to allow the normal rule of plurality of political parties and political bodies within their territory.

Granted the need of a body of the temporal order which shall set itself to recast the existing social régime in accordance with the principles of authentic humanism, it follows from the line of thinking we have pursued that such a body will answer to this description ; a party, or better, a political society which will not seek to group Catholics together as such or all Catholics but only *some* Catholics having such a conception as we have given of the historical ideal to be pursued and of the means to be employed in its pursuit : a party which will not seek to be exclusively Catholic or indeed exclusively Christian, but which will welcome all those who are in fact willing to devote themselves to a definite enterprise in history-making. That this enterprise is based in turn on scholastic metaphysic and Catholic spirituality, and that it calls accordingly for Catholic leadership is another matter. It must be true to its own nature, and in the fullest measure ; this being granted, the venture calls for the co-operation of every worker of good will.

Such a body operating (if it ever should come into existence) in the temporal order of political and social affairs should be invited to approach its task as a thing in essence spiritual and to use for its weapons the arms of Christian heroism—that is, of sanctity. Those only will be astonished at the apparent paradox who fail to appreciate the intrinsic and essential dependence of temporal on spiritual things ; and who do not see that the evils of which mankind is suffering in our time are incurable if divine principles and remedies are not applied to the deep sources of human life and of the profane and secular order. Of old God raised up saints to be military chiefs and leaders of the people, emperors or kings. Why should not He raise up others who shall be political leaders in the circumstances of our day or of the days to come ?

ON WAYS AND MEANS

6. We have said that in the ordinary course it is principally by its sincerity or single-mindedness that an effort at reform or revolution is made effective and that it has a chance of success in the actual order of things. But how is this possible in the case of an effort to renew the temporal order on Christian principles, an effort whose sincerity is by definition the sincerity of Christian principles, of the Gospel and of Charity, opposed to the sincerity

151

of violence, fanaticism or of hatred by which revolutions are known to succeed ? The purity or sincerity of ordinary revolution is apt to accommodate itself to much moral defilement. The purity and sincerity of an attempt to renew the temporal order on Christian principles excludes all ways and means that are not sincere and pure.

For this reason and by hypothesis is any attempt at reform that follows the Christian law foredoomed to failure ?

The question might need no other answer than the word of the Gospel : " The Son of Man, when He cometh, shall He find, think you, faith on earth ? " [1] A Christian revolution can succeed only by the use of just those means which are beyond the ability of others to use. If Faith is able to move mountains, is it powerless to shift the mighty from their seats ? If Christians, who live by Faith in their private lives, lay aside their faith when they approach the things of political and social life, they must be content to be towed like slaves in the wake of history.

Those who labour to transform the social order in the name of human personality and of Christian justice lay themselves open to reproach from two opposite poles. On the one hand they are accused of playing false to the proletariat by shrinking from violence and revolutionary force ; on the other hand they are accused of betraying the social order by making themselves harbingers of a revolution that will lay all things low.

This twofold reproach, though it be unjust,

[1] Luke, xviii. 8.

carries a warning. Nature has no forgiveness for those who fail to fulfil the law of their being ; and the Christian has to look to a very high plane for the laws that govern his life and action and that segregate him in the social order alike from the apostles of a revolution born of hate and from the representatives of an order based on avarice.

7. The theologians have worked out, often enough under pressure of events in history, a wise and balanced doctrine of the measure of resistance that may be offered to unjust law and tyranny, and of the measure of force that may be used in the establishment and execution of the law. We know that the political order and the temporal State are unable to do without the use of coercive force ; and that the spiritual power has equally the right in certain defined cases to use a measure of coercion ; and that force must always be employed as an instrument of justice ; for otherwise a great kingdom would be no better than a band of brigands. We also know that obedience must never be given to laws that contravene the commandments of God and that it is not only permissible to offer an active constitutional resistance to a tyrannical government (for instance to endeavour by constitutional means to change the existing political order) but also that citizens may have the duty not in their capacity as private individuals but under a mandate (at least tacit) of the people to apply passive resistance and even armed and open force (by way of defensive action) against the aggression of a lawful government turned tyrant and sometimes even to remove the

government[1] or to substitute a new authority in place of one which fails in face of a grave danger ; or again to oppose by violence even to the shedding of blood the succession to power of an usurper, always provided in such cases that the course proposed is not certain to bring greater evils to the commonwealth.

All this teaching is true and valuable. But, in fact, is it only in this way, by reference to the conditions that are requisite to justify the use of force, that the question arises in our time ? Be these rules ever so necessary, do the means of action to which they relate constitute a sufficient equipment for the Christian who is engaged in the conflict of our time ?

The question raised by the condition of the temporal order in our time does not concern the action of a tyrant laying a city to waste by cruelty and rapine and thus disturbing the normal course of human life and things that ordinarily jog along in the common way of the world. The question that confronts our time has to do with a universal state of depression and disorder. It has to do with the birth of a new world out of the womb of history in the travail of a crisis of unexampled severity. The peoples of the earth are face to face with an

---

[1] Cf. St. Thomas Aquinas, *Summa theol.*, ii–ii, 42. 2. ad 3. " To appreciate this teaching it is well to bear in mind that in contradistinction to the Sovereign Pontiff, who is not Vicar of the Church but is Vicar of Christ, the King is Vicar of the People, *vices gerens multitudinis*. The Constituent Power is the appanage of the People, the King has only a power of Regency or of rule. Cf. *Summa theol.*, i–ii, 90. 3, with the commentary of Fr. Billot in *De Ecclesia Christi* (Rome, 1921 ; p. 293)." C. Journet, Preface to *Le Gouvernement Royal* (De Reg. Principum), Paris, 1931, Librairie du Dauphin.

order of things that is in truth apocalyptic : the Pope has warned them that not since the days of Noah has mankind known such a scale of evil.

Moreover, and this is the critical matter that should, we think, command all our attention—the circumstances of the modern world raise in the sharpest possible way the problems that surround the use of revolutionary violence and of coercive force. A prime issue for a long time obscured or rejected in face of makeshift solutions of an empirical sort comes into full view : In the political and social struggle that is the eternal lot of human society and more particularly in the conflict concerning the very basis of social life that is called forth by periods of revolutionary change, has the Christian ethic nothing else to offer to those who are engaged in temporal strife than abstract advice to moderate and limit in accordance with the rules of reason and of divine law the use of coercive force or of revolutionary violence as the case may be ? Or, more generally—and without using the word in its pejorative sense—abstract advice as to the use of the means of secular warfare ? If it is really so, is there not an inevitable conflict between the demands of Christian ethics and of temporal success so that, more especially in periods of barbarism, of universal barbarism, of barbarism of technique, of barbarism on the titanic scale, the Christian soul, lost in hopeless perplexity, is obliged in fact to elect between strict adherence to its own ethic and a successful course of secular action which is forbidden by the same ethic ? Is the Christian soul doomed to defeat if it remains loyal ; to infidelity if it declares for success ? Or, as an alternative, to perpetual inaction ?

To moderate force is to render it less forceful ; to restrain and curb the energy of revolution (not by way of technical regulation as a matter of art directed to an end to be attained, but by the rules of ethics, the prescriptions of virtue and the requirements of the last end of our human life) is to diminish that energy and to deny oneself the aid of many useful means. It follows that the man of least scruple is the most certain of success. Is the spirit therefore by hypothesis condemned to pusillanimity in the things of time ? Are its energies without influence in the order of the world save by way of the repercussion of Eternity on Time ? Is the spirit of man which abides at the centre of the temporal and social and political order and of their conflict, doomed for ever to impotence and to perpetual failure ?

That is a piece of Manichean not of Christian thinking, which is not to say that it has been absent from the philosophy of history that has guided the practice of the Christian world. It is one thing to know that the things of time are subject to corruption and that natural and supernatural law make fertile on a higher plane what is failure in the temporal order ; and quite another thing to abandon for ever to the Devil the world and the things of time. The Christian knows that the work of the spirit though often thwarted and often obscure makes constant progress in time ; and as one failure follows on another, one secret gain is yet added to another, and Time goes forward to the Resurrection, and the history of the world always moves towards the Eternal Jerusalem.

8. When an age in which the forces of the spirit led to the consecration of secular things and the arms of violence and of appetite even in the secular order gives way to an age of reflexion, Christian civilisation tends in truth to dissolve. The things of man pull one way, the things of God another way, as in the Lutheran system do faith and works ; and in the system of Molina, grace and freedom.   Christian Europe, having lost its simple faith and not yet recovered in consciousness the wisdom and understanding of the Incarnation, and being attacked in its vital centres by an alien humanism which was nurtured at its breast and later sought to destroy it, reacted again in a similar fashion.   It is the age of the Protestant Reformation and of the successes of Puritanism, the age of the Counter Reformation and of the Concordats.   Dualism, which heresy promoted and encouraged and which the Church fought even while endeavouring to adjust herself to its existence, is one of the characteristic features of this age.

The result was almost inevitable. Whilst on one plane of activity the Church concluded concordats with secular Powers, on another plane of life and thought the Christian world, Catholic and Protestant, made terms with sin.   It was an instructive exchange of greeting between Machiavellian immorality and Lutheran pessimism. A sharing, a division of labour was gradually established and appeared in full view in the bourgeois world of the period after

157

the French Revolution. The soul of man, desirous of finding salvation in peace with God, lays on the State or more generally on the institutions of political and social life the duty of insuring with the Devil its temporal security and progress.

And thus the instruments of force and of temporal power that the Middle Ages had essayed to sanctify were abandoned without moral sanction to the law of their fleshly inclination. And rich Puritans and other devout persons gave to the Creator of worldly goods the worship that is His due while they received in good (and very good) conscience the fruits of the toil of women and of children, of the *sweating system* and the other systems of moneygetting that disgraced the early decades of the nineteenth century. And so the spiritual (not the real thing but its sociological *phenomenon*) seemed incapable of success in the world and capable of holding its ground and of making some progress in the temporal order only in league with iniquity. Like the pious Jewish housewife who employs a *goi* servant so that the housework may be done on the Sabbath, this pharasaical spirituality relied on political forces to do the work that its scruples forbade it to do. In this way the action of States as well as the conduct of wars and conspiracies, revolutions, acts of violence and the rest came to be the work of a tiny group of men who sacrificed their virtue on the altar of public welfare in much the same way that prostitutes sacrifice their honour to maintain the peace of families.

It is to be hoped that the new age of which the first rays are beginning to reach us may be—I mean for Christians and for Christianity however it may befall the children of the world—an age not of theocracy or of humanism, but an age more human than humanism and more divine than theocracy[1]; an age in which the dignity and the nobility of creation will be more than ever recognised but in the measure in which creatures are of God and in which He lives in them : humanism, yes, but a humanism of the Incarnation ; theocracy, yes, but a theocracy of divine love inhabiting the heart. In any event it seems that the dualism and the separation of which we have spoken have run their course. The progress of evil and of sin in the heart of our civilisation makes it plain to Christians in a way that brooks no denial that certain apportionments of office and of responsibility are impossible.

9. In relation to the State we wrote elsewhere[2] "States nowadays have turned their methods of existence into an organised system of sin." For one who honestly faces the problem of a Christian State in our time (I mean a State that is in truth and not in an ornamental sense Christian) the question of a complete reform of the State is thus inevitable ; of reform, that is to say, conceived not on the lines that Calvin followed at Geneva, when he asked from the State a greater measure of virtue than is proper to its nature ; but requiring at any

---

[1] We speak of theocracy in a general sense and to indicate a moral attitude. Strictly speaking, medieval Christianity never professed theocracy in the political sense, since it always affirmed the distinction between the two Powers.

[2] *Primauté du Spirituel*, p. 132. *The Things that are not Caesar's*, p. 85.

rate that the principle of the lesser evil be honestly applied, and that the State itself do not make sin one of its instruments. Justice is of greater value than force in the conservation of the State, and, even when they are disciplined by Justice, the means of coercion in the hands of an authority which is entitled to compel obedience and which is able to control the machinery of the modern State represent a secular force that is formidable enough in all conscience.

10. In the case of those who are engaged in a struggle with *the* State or with *a* State for a just cause in the temporal order, and above all in the case of those who take a revolutionary stand against a particular régime, the question that arises if they are Christians, or more generally if they make an appeal to the things of the spirit and to the dignity of human personality, is not simply one of the ethical control of the means of secular struggle. The issue is as to the worth of this whole order of means. In truth technical progress has grown so perfect that modern political warfare has come to involve a regular mobilisation of all the devils of the human heart. And success is bought by those means only at this price. We are far from the time of Harmodius and of Aristogeiton and far from the time of rioting and barricades. Revolutions, at any rate in the crisis of action and at the moment of seizure of power (for afterwards the appetite grows) are effected nowadays in kid gloves and with a minimum of bloodshed. But as it means the setting in motion on an extended front of an immense

mass of public opinion and of public passion, it becomes necessary on a scale that grows increasingly more vast to provoke a violent agitation of the public mind and conscience. The wretchedness and humiliation that overwhelm men must be turned to hatred, to the need of victims in expiation, to the unloosing of pride of race, of class, of nation. But bold and fearless falsehood, falsehood sure of itself, fast as the pillars of Hercules, unshakeable as the rock of truth, becomes the power *par excellence* that is demanded for the manufacture of political opinion. *Fortitudo martyrum !* The proper preparation of the mass of human material for political warfare means that the whole people shall be nurtured on fable and steeped in imposture ; that they shall be taught to call good evil and evil good, and shall be clothed in the plaster cast of stupidity of which specimens are offered to us in the racial propaganda of one and the atheist propaganda of another power of our time. It is a mass of people so prepared that has to involve its conscience and assume responsibility for the crimes of history. *Galeam salutis assumite et gladium spiritus.* Put ye on the arms of falsehood, take in hand the shield of infatuation and cover yourselves with the helmet of cruelty. Ye Christians who are now at the end of your powers, who think ye are revolutionaries with good cause but who are not revolutionary enough, since ye believe in many human fables and the true revolutionary is one who believes in God alone, ye hapless lambs against whom the hand of slaughter is already raised and who seek to roar, look at the enemies with whom ye have to deal and ask yourselves if it is even conceivable that you can defeat them with the arms they use. They have brought dishonour on Force. In their hands Force, I mean material force, that was once the arm of the Spirit, is now no better than violence and brutality. Watch them harry their miserable folk by whipping up a domesticated fervour of fear and of illusion. Never has man been more degraded and disfigured, never has the spirit that envies him even before he is born held him so completely up to ridicule.

So long as one sticks solely to the instruments of secular warfare, one is inevitably led in existing circumstances to the use of a technique of this kind. And it is reasonable enough that such a technique should be employed in the course of revolutions in which everything is sacrificed to social and temporal ends. But in the case of a revolution which makes its appeal in the name of human personality, of spiritual order, of Christian values, can it be so ? The thing would involve a flagrant contradiction. Of late, the observation was made not without reason, that certain revolutionaries who appeal to human personality seem strangely to hold personality or at any rate popular personality in contempt. Thus one of them writes : " The revolution uses all kinds of things to feed its fire. Envy, hatred, fear blaze up more fiercely than love. A good revolutionary technique turns the basest passions to the service of the common weal." And another says : " I fully appreciate that no ideology will win success if it is unable to supply of itself a picture coarse enough and simple enough to please the crowd. . . . An ethic of revolt must necessarily be an improvised and in some ways a barbarous ethic."

" Such utterances are not agreeable to the Christian conscience " is the comment of the young Catholic from whom we borrow the citations.[1]

For these reasons indifference to the means or instruments of action would be a serious error on the part of those who declare themselves revolution-aries in the name of the spirit. One who claims such patronage has no right to say that " the technical means that are used in effecting the revolution are of little consequence, provided only that the revolu-tion takes place." A representative of a new political body once said : " It (meaning the new political force) acting at first perhaps in alliance with Com-munism will effect the collectivist revolution. But this revolution will be merely destructive, an elimina-tion of profiteers. It will then proceed to bring about the revolution which shall be the restoration of personal values. This latter revolution will be the true constructive revolution " ; and so forth. Texts like these prove to demonstration that good will is not enough ; let alone naïveté.

Et propter vitam vivendi perdere causas. If those who desire to work towards a transformation of the temporal régime on the basis of Christian principles and *personal* values do not face fully and squarely and with an appreciation of all the moral issues that are involved the problem of instruments and means that may be used, the reform

---

[1] Raymond de Becker : *Christianisme et Révolution,* Vie Intellectuelle, 25 June, 1933.

they desiderate will lose in the process of realisation its whole *raison d'être*. The means to be used must of necessity be consonant with the end in view. The establishment of a régime that shall be worthy of the rational nature of man and oriented to his freedom of autonomy postulates the use of means that are worthy of his rational nature and that are consonant with such freedom. The position of those who desire in this world of flesh and blood and time to fulfil the demands of the spirit by the exclusive use of the instruments of secular conflict is now untenable. Either they are driven to the immoderate use of the means of secular conflict and to the rejection of their own ideals, or they are compelled to recognise the necessity of having recourse to means of a different order.

11. And here it is essential to expose what may be called the myth of insurrection, the idea (associated more or less consciously in the minds of many with the word revolution) that great operations in the temporal order and great historical changes and revolutions are always and necessarily operations of war or insurrection against a certain established order or disorder ; that they consist in essence in the destruction or removal of some obstacle. Caesarian operations of the latter kind are sometimes necessary. But ordinarily the fact that the unborn child has reached its term causes the forces of nature to open the maternal womb for its delivery. Great events of history and great revolutions normally result from a hidden process of growth, from the internal thrust of a new order which takes form and

shape and fulfils its own ontological requirements within the heart of a given state of civilisation.

Such a process is more natural than artificial, the part that human surgery plays being much less than it appears in the operation of revolt. None the less it calls for an incomparably greater expenditure of human energy and human effort. The means it uses are not those of warfare, of struggle with an enemy who has to be overcome or with an obstacle that has to be destroyed ; they are rather means of organic construction (following the parallels of embryology) ; the struggle is a struggle towards the being and existence of new life and its growth and establishment in the real order.

These are the means *par excellence* that are proper to a renewal of the temporal order on Christian principles. These are the prime means that the Christian ethic proposes to all who are engaged in the conflict of our time ; secular means or spiritual means, " rich temporal means " or " poor temporal means "[1] disposed and disciplined by the spirit, these are *par excellence* the means of construction for Christian use because the Christian has a natural love of Being and a natural desire to co-operate with the push of creative forces at the heart of history, and because means of this kind naturally desiderate in the agents who use them a secret anonymity, the *Non nobis Domine* that the heart of the pagan finds it so difficult to achieve. Christians have experience in the course of history of many more successes and achievements than would appear on the surface of things since they are achievements in

[1] See above, p. 133.

165

the order of which we are speaking, in the order of organic construction, and are masked in some sense by the nature of the means by which they are produced. The fractures they make (which is the thing most visible and most sensible to human eyes and interests) happen in fact at points more or less distant from the centre of operation of the means by which they are produced, and appear to men as simple effects, not as ends immediately intended. It is thus in the natural order of things that the glory that goes with visible results should pass to those who prefer to employ methods of violence rather than means of organic or moral reconstruction. Since methods of violence are in use and operation at the very moment of change or revolution, and the immediate aim of these methods is to make a breach or fracture at the point where the activity of man appears in the full light of day, it is natural that the spirit should appear to suffer defeat when " man the enemy " comes and steals its wage and hoists upon the works it has prepared the colours of violence and evil. But such a defeat is defeat in appearance only. Many of the failures of Christianity have been seeming failures only ; and in fact were hidden or disguised successes.

The spirit is not doomed to pusillanimity in time ; the Christian soul is not locked in an irremediable perplexity ; the conflict between the claims of ethics and those of temporal success is only an apparent conflict, for the ways of organic or moral reconstruction have in truth more potency in promoting historical change than the ways of war, and in particular the means of secular warfare by reference to which this conflict and this perplexity have arisen. It is, first and foremost, by bringing into being in the very centre of the existing temporal régime the institutions proper to a new order of things, the truths upon which that order depends, the organic shapes in which it begins to take existence, that Christian men and women can work within the temporal system towards renewal of the face of the earth and the destruction of the existing disorder.

And yet, are the conflict and the perplexity of which we have spoken, are they *entirely* removed ? Means of warfare, though not in themselves the most important, are none the less necessary. The history of mankind does not in fact dispense with these means. Chiefly it is true in the shape of military wars, conflicts of peoples and invasions of territory, but also in acts of violence and political revolution, these means often play a decisive rôle in the last phases of historical change. In times of great crisis it seems less easy than ever to avoid the use of violence. If the Christian is not doomed to failure pure and simple, is he at any rate and especially in our time doomed to the appearance of failure ? Are the arms of moral reconstruction the only arms he is at liberty to use ? In face of the technique of secular struggle that the modern world has elaborated, is he denied the use of these means of warfare ? This problem also claims attention but it can only be dealt with by way of hypothesis.

Vis fugere a Deo ? Fuge in Deum. So spoke Augustine. If any one, led astray by history as the positivists narrate it, is tempted to give way before the apparent ineptitude of the spirit in the things of time, let him go forward and enter into the very depths of the spirit, and learn its power not only in the things of eternity but also in the things of time ; not only over the soul but over the flesh also. There are other means of warfare than secular means. If a spiritual means could furnish arms of sufficient strength, the debate would shift its axis, and the possibility of fresh solutions would appear.

Spiritual and Secular Means of Warfare

12. At this point it is opportune to examine the evidence that is afforded by Gandhi. This evidence is of special significance for Christians, to whom it recalls not merely in theory, but through suffering and self-sacrifice, truths that it is their mission to cultivate and bring to fruition. We have already written that " the example of Gandhi should put us to shame ! "[1] Not that it ought to be taken in an uncritical spirit or without reserve ; but it is heart-breaking to hear Catholics talk of Gandhi with levity and contempt and to find a press which is said to be right-minded covering him with sarcasm and ridicule.

If the methods adopted by Gandhi have any value, why should Christians not lay hold of the elements of good they contain ? True, they have received the word of divine revelation ; but they

---

[1] *Primauté du Spirituel,* p. 31 ; *The Things that are not Caesar's,* 85.

have not a monopoly of truth. To take and to refine every truth that is spoken in any part of the human household is an essential law of Christian life and action. It follows from the idea of Catholicity that every just man of non-Christian denomination belongs to the invisible unity of the Church and on this ground only has a title to salvation ; and it accordingly behoves the members of the visible Church to welcome every work of justice that is done on earth as a contribution to the common good. Such an attitude of welcome verily involves an interior struggle on every front and an exact formation on all points of doctrine, if they are to possess and not to be possessed, if they are to lead others into the unity of truth and not to be led away into the errors of syncretism.

And now imagine the depth of the folly of those Catholics, priests and laymen (truth to tell they are mostly priests and young priests), who are occupied (in the elegant style of modern young men who like to defer coming to a conclusion) in depriving souls of their spiritual arms and in detaching them (as if it were a futile scholasticism) from the inspired wisdom of the Common Doctor of the Church.

13. Not only would *Satyagraha* be inapplicable in its original form to countries outside India without recasting and entire readaptation ; but it also needs rectification on essential points. Gandhi has no sense of the State. Instead of retaining it in existence and calling for its subordination to a superior order he seems to condemn in principle and absolutely the use of force by the executive,

and in a general way the use of every secular instrument of power. And thus he seems not wholly to escape an *angelism* which carried to its extreme limit involves (as every *angelism* does) the rejection of the Incarnation, and presupposes also a radical misunderstanding of human nature. Hence the weakness of his system. It is capable of achieving partial results of great importance and of changing little by little the moral atmosphere of a people, of teaching a people to become conscious of its own selfhood, and of putting collective energies into operation with most powerful effect. And yet by reason of its refusal to adopt a policy at once more human and more rational, it lacks the power to register in history broad political results or to remodel the temporal régime in an organic way; so that at the moment of approach to decisive action the energies it had called into existence are in danger of being dissipated or (what would be for it the worst kind of failure) of being converted to violence and anarchy.

But this criticism is valid only against the use of *spiritual means* and of *poor temporal means*[1] to the exclusion of all other means. The technique of Gandhi if translated to the intellectual climate of a truer and more realist philosophy would retain all its truth and lose all its exclusiveness. One may wonder if with the necessary rectification and readaptation, it could not (as Gandhi has often declared) be applied in the West as it has been in the East; and give new life to the temporal struggle for freedom and human personality.

[1] See p. 133, *supra.*

There will be found in an Appendix at the end of this book a note edited in 1924 by Gandhi himself on the doctrine of *Satyagraha,* which gives an authentic account of the doctrine as it was elaborated little by little in the course of some thirty years of experience. It will be seen that while, to some extent and no doubt under the influence of Tolstoy, he wrongly rejects all use of coercive force (which he confounds with violence[1]), he affirms with an emphasis that demands our serious attention, the value of the " Power of Love " and the " Power of the Soul " and the " Power of Truth " as instruments and means of political and social action ; " patience and voluntary suffering, the vindication of truth not by inflicting suffering on our opponent but on our own self " being " the arms of the bravest of the brave." " *Satyagraha* is self-dependent. It does not require the assent of our opponent before being brought into play. Indeed it manifests its power most strongly against an opponent who offers resistance. It is therefore irresistible. A *Satyagrahi* does not know what defeat is, for he fights for truth without losing any of his strength. Death in the struggle is release and prison a gateway wide open to liberty. . . . And as a *Satyagrahi* never injures his adversary and always appeals either to his reason by gentle argument or to his heart by sacrifice of self, *Satyagraha* is twice blessed ; it blesses him who practises it and him against whom it is put in practice."

[1] The word *violence* used by Gandhi is equivocal. One may not use violence towards an adversary to " impose the truth " on him. But the common good may call for the use of force against those who put *it* in peril.

Let us then be just to Gandhi, even while we note his errors and remain on guard against the tendencies to idealism and unrealism that are inherent in his doctrine. Another philosophy will furnish us with the key to a rational solution.

It is, we think, of capital importance at this point to recur to the true doctrine of Force or Fortitude, considered as a power of the soul or moral virtue. Every act of fortitude is obviously not virtue. But fortitude is a cardinal virtue in so far as it inclines and steadies the will of man to meet and overcome difficulties that are in conflict with the claims of justice and with the life of reason and of truth.[1] Fortitude being thus directed to the firm and loyal defence of right against every kind of evil, its proper object is to prepare the soul for the sake of justice to meet death.[2]

And here is something that goes to the root of the problem that we are investigating : the principal act of the virtue of fortitude is not, in the teaching of St. Thomas,[3] the act of attacking, *aggredi*, but the act of enduring, bearing, suffering with constancy, *sustinere*. Aristotle had already observed in the third book of the Ethics : *in sustinendo tristitias maxime aliqui fortes dicuntur*. To repress fear and to overcome terror, to remain steadfast in the midst of peril, facing evils that already make you feel the bane and that will endure and yet seem already to be beyond your strength; this needs more character than the control of anger and audacity that are apt to launch you suddenly, buoyed up with hope, towards a peril of your own making.

[1] St. Thomas Aquinas, *Summa theol.*, ii–ii, 123. 1.
[2] *Ibid.* 4.   [3] *Ibid.* 6.

This distinction governs the whole issue under discussion. If there is given to the term warfare (as St. Thomas does in the article under consideration) a sense as wide as analogy will allow, and if one nominates in a general way as means of warfare, in public and in private life, all the means that mankind uses in opposition and in conflict to overcome an obstacle or to resist an overwhelming force, one is led to reflect that there are two orders of means of warfare (taken in the widest sense of the word) as there are two kinds of fortitude and of courage, the courage that attacks and the courage that endures, the force of coercion or aggression and the force of patience, the force that inflicts suffering on others and the force that endures suffering inflicted on oneself. There you have two different keyboards that stretch along the two sides of our human nature though the sounds they give are constantly intermingled. And if it be true that there is no redemption without shedding of blood there can only be in the last analysis these two orders of means in the conflict against evil in the world : the one that leads to shedding, if need be, of the blood of others ; the other which leads to the sacrifice of one's own life.

The first of these orders derives its efficacy in the last resort from the body and from the transitive activity that is proper to matter : the second derives its efficacy from the soul and from the immanent activity that is proper to the spirit.[1] We may

[1] To the objection " Majoris potentiae esse videtur quod aliquid possit in aliud agere quam quod ipsum ab alio non immutetur. Sed aggredi est in aliud agere, sustinere autem est immobiliter perseverare. Cum · ergo fortitudo perfectionem

173

say then that the first of these orders of means is related to secular means of a particular genre (namely as means of warfare) and the second—even when its immediate aim is a temporal end—has relation to spiritual means also of a particular genre (again, as a means of warfare).[1] For this reason the use of *courage in endurance* corresponds to the principal act of the virtue of fortitude and is characteristic of the " brave of the brave." Such endurance derives its strength from something that possesses the greatest power of resistance in the world of nature, from the paradox of a nothing which is also a universe, the invisible power of human personality. Other kinds of courage derive their strength from something that may equally serve or destroy personality, namely the energies of the material and measurable world. It goes without saying that means of endurance like means of aggression may be used as well for evil as for good ends. The devil has his martyrs too. But it is noteworthy that aggressive action naturally tends to find its fullest expression in the unloosing of the

---

potentiae nominet, videtur quod magis ad fortitudinem pertineat aggredi quam sustinere " St. Thomas answers : " Sustinere importat quidem passionem corporis ; sed actum animae fortissime inhaerentis bono, ex quo sequitur quod non cedat passioni corporali jam imminenti. Virtus autem magis attenditur circa animam quam circa corpus." *Summa theol.*, ii–ii, 123. 6. ad. 2.

[1] In another book (*Religion and Culture*, pp. 49–51) I draw a distinction between "rich temporal means " and " poor temporal means." This distinction, which involves a different point of view (see above, p. 133), does not coincide exactly with the distinction that is drawn between ' secular ' and ' spiritual ' means. The distinction between the use of courage in attack and courage in endurance refers to the latter distinction in the particular case of means of " warfare."

forces of nature and of passion under the control of an intelligence which proceeds on purely technical principles unfettered by any consideration of Divine or natural law, so much so indeed that the moral rules of reason and of love tend to limit and reverse the operation of those forces whose native urge takes no note of the nature of man. On the other hand, means of endurance tend to find their fullest expression in the sovereign freedom of a soul that is exalted above the terrors of nature and of death and enveloped in the sacred fire of Uncreated Holiness, so that these means tend of themselves to follow the moral rules of reason and of love. Love is the animating principle of the spiritual means of warfare ; their power is verily the power of love. Merely human love and even misguided love is able to overcome obstacles of the most difficult kind. Shall not the power of these means be still more mighty if the love that governs their action is essentially sane, spiritual, noble, rid of all egoism and base passion ; if its source and its end be Truth : if its name be Charity ?

15. The force of coercion and of aggression, the force that strikes, aims at the destruction of one evil by way of another evil (in the physical order) which it inflicts on the body. It follows that evil (on however small a scale) passes from one to other endlessly according to the law of transitive action. For the patient, unless he has understood and voluntarily *accepted* the hurt he has received— which happens rarely and anyhow depends on strength of soul—is stirred to react in more or less

crafty ways of evil-doing. The force of voluntary suffering and of patience, the force of endurance, tends to annihilate the evil by accepting and dissolving it in love, sublimating its sorrow in the soul in the shape of resignation. There it stays, and goes no further. And thus the force that strikes and is necessary and, if it be just, stops the expansion of evil and limits and contracts but is unable to extinguish it, has in its own nature less strength and perfection than the force that endures and that, in the case where it is informed by Charity, is of its own strength capable of extinguishing as it arises the evil that free agents unnecessarily introduce into the world. It is evidently of its own nature a more effective instrument of redemption.

The type *par excellence* of the force that strikes, of courage in attack, is the power of the conqueror ; the type of warfare in which such force is exerted is military war for one's country.[1] The Sword is the noblest symbol of the means that are used in war. The Cross is the supreme symbol of the force that endures, of the courage that suffers. Even though it be unawares, all those who fight with these arms are drawn towards the Cross. This kind of force finds its highest type in the fortitude of the martyrs ; the type of war in which it is exerted in the struggle of the saint for heaven : *estote fortes in bello*.

And thus the debate that engages our attention, the debate between secular and spiritual means, is in the last analysis the issue between the Cross and

[1] This is why the language of revolutionaries who are most hostile to the army and to their country is always and invariably the language of military metaphor : they cannot escape the ascendancy of military warfare and of victory.

the Sword. The Cross stretches out its arms over spiritual things and hence over temporal things also. The Sword puts its steel at the service of the temporal power and, by virtue of a natural subordination, at the service of the Spiritual Power also. Heir of the Roman Empire and of systems of civilisation with a strong political life, the Christian West has not failed to appreciate that even in relation to spiritual ends the sword and material means may be used, within the limits of justice. Even St. Augustine in the end admitted that against the destruction wrought by heretics the Church might appeal to the material power of the secular arm. The Church again, being a perfect society, is entitled in her own sphere to exercise a certain measure of coercion.

In systems of civilisation that might almost be said to be a-political, as in India, it is on the other hand more easy, almost too easy, to suppose that even in relation to ends of the temporal order spiritual means might be employed. Not that they have ever ignored this truth to whom the mystery of the Cross has been revealed : the whole conduct of the Christian life is the practice and the illustration of it. The way of the Cross is the way of wisdom not only in our spiritual life but also in the temporal order. But the question that more particularly concerns us here is whether spiritual means may not constitute a special type of arm that may be used in the political and the social order. Gandhi has shown his originality in the separation and the systematic organisation of patience and voluntary suffering as a special method of political activity.

Whether they follow the method of Gandhi or some other method which has yet to be invented, men who attach importance to spiritual values and whom Western civilisation and in particular the Catholic Church have put on their guard against the errors of idealism and of false mysticism are likely to be led willy-nilly to a solution along these lines, if it be true that secular means of warfare are less and less capable of claiming the first place in their thought, either because the weapons to be used have fallen into the hands of the enemy or because those means of warfare can now ensure success only through the agency of sin. It is possible in these circumstances that new modes of political activity may make their appearance. Such a possibility, we think, ought not to be excluded on *a priori* grounds, for the political order is essentially a human order directed towards the good of our temporal life and towards the accomplishment of a human task ; and it has its effects on the bodies and on the souls of men. In the temporal conflicts that are waged within the State it would be unnatural to expect that secular means should play no part. But it would be unnatural to expect that spiritual means should not also play their part. And if secular means of conflict have developed a special technique, may not spiritual means of warfare do the like ? [1]

---

[1] Aiming at the destruction of the enemy, the whole technique of military warfare, on the other hand, is by definition confined to the domain of secular means and of aggressive force. And yet, here again it is in the *sustinere* of one who offers his body to immediate death, as in the case of Psichari, that the virtue of fortitude finds its highest expression. And the technique of the defensive in warfare is more difficult, and also more important than that of the offensive.

16.   If it is true that the social life of the Christian is inseparable from his spiritual life, so that Christian heroism is necessarily to be found at the basis of a reconstruction of the social system on Christian principles, would not modes of political action that have their origin in the Power of Love be preferable and more in accord with the work of sanctity that a reconstruction of the temporal order on Christian lines presupposes and requires ?   And those also (even though they be not Christians) who desire to effect a revolution that will restore *personal* values, ought not they to put those means of action in the first rank of the means they use, seeing that they are more consonant with the dignity and the power that are proper to rational beings ?   Would not such means of action, which do not aim at destruction of public authority, but which call on it to act unjustly or to desist from action, enable men more easily to reconcile the general obligation of obedience to established authority that is laid upon the Christian conscience (saving only certain special cases of tyranny and so forth that we have already mentioned[1]) with the extended possibilities of political struggle in our own time ?

Again.   If means of endurance and voluntary suffering correspond to the principal act of the virtue of fortitude, what in turn are their power and efficacy in the physical order, in external reality ? Little or nothing ?   Though this power is less apparent and adapted rather to laying the deep foundations of after events, there is we believe reason to think that it may in truth be of equal importance with the

[1] See p. 153.

power of aggression and coercion—I mean on its own plane and without pretending to take the place of the latter in their proper field of action. Imagine a political group of men who decide to resume (though in a different form, since they must have recourse to means of political warfare) and to transpose into the temporal order the methods of the early Christians and of apostles of all times. They make use especially of the measures that we have nominated measures of organic reconstruction, seeking, for instance, without reference to the struggle between the several parties for control of the government of the State, to bring into existence among the people new modes and organs of economic and political life.[1] But they go beyond the ordinary means that the law provides and that are not, strictly speaking, means of warfare. In cases where it becomes necessary they carry on their campaign by voluntary suffering, they practise poverty, they endure punishment carrying the loss of civil rights, they go out to meet these things, shouting the truth in season and out of season, refusing in certain cases to co-operate with the civil authority, and initiating reforms outside the law, not to disorganise the State or to imperil its safety[2] but to obtain the repeal of an unjust law, or to bear

[1] We may refer, as a very special instance, to the curious attempt at land colonization that is being made by the Distributists in England.

[2] Apart from the fact that the systematic refusal to render military service, such as is practised by Conscientious Objectors, is based on an ideology that is shallow and steeped in illusion, it is also of no real effect against the evil of warfare and might well endanger the safety of the community in a case where a just war had to be waged.

witness to the existence of a right, to force a reform of which reason has recognised the necessity, to prepare little by little the transformation of the temporal régime, until the hour comes when the burden of office and responsibility shall fall into the hands of the group. All these visible acts in the external order are for the actors no more than occasions of spiritual trial and adjustment in a life whose aim is the perfection of the soul. In the achievement of these ends and in the patient acceptance of the ill treatment they are made to suffer, they try to be without hatred and without pride; they exert a stern measure of self-control so as not to be wanting in justice, and they do not allow falsehood or anything else that degrades man to dishonour their action; they truly love those against whom they are fighting as they truly love those for whom they are fighting; all the evil that is done to them is engulfed in their charity; before they bear witness against evil, love has consumed the evil in their heart. Their influence on the world is great, because by suffering injustice in cases in which the injustice must sooner or later be avenged on earth, they oblige Providence in a manner of speaking to take their side; because their charity heaps up on the heads of their enemies coals of fire that cancel out ill-will or chastens it; and again because the power of love is a radiant energy that convinces men and carries them with it. If love is expressed in a visible form, the radiation of this form will be out of all proportion to its intrinsic power.

To one who contemplates the circumstances of our own time, the power of hate may seem more overwhelming. In truth the stakes are not even. To make the comparison fair the love of the wise would have to be as intense as the hatred of fools; and we know it rarely happens so. . . .

And yet, if one looks at the thing in itself, away from this or that concrete historical circumstance, it does not seem altogether impossible that many may be led by their enthusiasm to wage the good fight with the arms of love and fortitude. Since such ways of action correspond to a high development of the virtue of fortitude, the majority of men are not able to attain to it of their own unaided strength; but they may be taught and guided: a work which might be done by a few heroic souls.

Besides, is it not a false prudence that hesitates to set before men and women tasks that are difficult of achievement? For many of those who are wont in speech to exalt the dignity of the human soul are apt in practice to despise it. It is a paradox of human nature that for all its weakness and wretchedness it responds more readily to a call to superhuman than to ordinary human effort. For the sake of some " mystical " cause of absolute value that is yet incarnate in contingent reality and experience the mass of men will suffer much evil and endure it with love in their heart. The history of social democracy in our time makes it plain to demonstration that without an ardent love of such a kind achievement is impossible.

The young bourgeois revolutionary brings to the revolution a demand for immediate success and the fussy positivism that are part of the habits of his class. But poverty schools men to appreciate the hidden efficacy of the ways of patience and of the courage that endures. For a whole century now the people of the West have been deflecting from its proper end and giving to the cause of materialist revolution an astonishing contribution of Christian virtue.

17. The tragedy of our time is precisely that this contribution has been made in the interests of materialist revolution, and that the initial error of the Christian world has led so many to think of Heaven as a Dome *de luxe* that shelters the life of the " Haves " and is reserved exclusively for their uses. During the *bourgeois* period the temporal apparatus that was used to translate (and to betray) religion on the sociological plane led the working masses to the reflexion : Religion is not for us. To this spiritual injury and the resentment of a wounded soul that retreated within itself were united not only the results of the preaching of the materialist revolutionary doctrine but also the results of a spontaneous operation of thought which slowly developed, in the shape of a mental attitude if not of a formulated system, a philosophy of life proper to the working classes and deeply rooted in visible and tangible reality.

In the upshot the language of the Christian faith has come to be for vast sections of the working classes something so alien that even to start a conversation is a serious problem. This state of affairs is one of the major difficulties that confronts every attempt to reconstruct the social order on a basis of Christian principles or, in a more general way, of the acknowledgment of absolute and supra-temporal values.

Let it be added, however, that to discount the importance of popular Christian elements would be an error, and that from these reserves of moral power it is not unlikely that active political formations may one day issue. It is to be noted too that the reserves of spiritual energy that are to be found in human nature may be liberated by preaching and example and set in operation in the hearts of many without any sense of spiritual things other than that which they may find in the concrete experience of the fight for justice here below. If every great social reform sets in motion obscure and elementary forces in the life of peoples, justice and love are also part and parcel of these forces. Many men strive for ends that are in line with justice before they reach any explicit understanding of religious truth : and would seem, simply from the angle of natural law and virtue, to be able to appreciate the value and the efficacy in temporal conflict of the spiritual instruments of patience and voluntary suffering.

18. In the last four paragraphs are set forth the reasons which in our opinion argue the possibility of using these instruments as a political arm. It is the man of action only who can demonstrate whether such a possibility can be fulfilled in the real and practical order. The means in question are spiritual means directed to temporal uses. Above them, in the hierarchy of absolute values, are purely spiritual means directed towards God, that are familiar in the religious technique of all the peoples of the earth and that the Gospel has hallowed with its supernatural authority : " This kind can go out

by nothing, but by prayer and fasting."[1] " Unless you shall do penance you shall all likewise perish."[2] We know that these means are of no value without charity and that before it acts in a more visible way love acts of its own impulse and with their virtuous aid in the secret kingdom of the Conscience and of God. We know too that it is by the blood of Christ applied throughout time that creation is redeemed from hour to hour so that the sacrifice of the Cross which is continued by every Mass that is celebrated on earth is by far the most excellent of all purely spiritual means.

As, however, they belong to different orders the means to which we refer cannot be used as substitutes one for another. Below purely spiritual means directed towards Eternity[3] come spiritual means that are directed to the things of Time and to worldly conflict. These spiritual means are incarnate in activities that have a temporal end, and especially in the activities that have been under discussion on an earlier page ; spiritual means of temporal warfare which depend above all on patience and the courage that endures, and in relation to which we have raised the question whether they might not give rise to a new technique of political action.

[1] Mark, ix. 28. [2] Luke, xiii. 3.
[3] A propos such purely spiritual means one may observe, with Cajetan, that they are " proper causes " of effects that are also spiritual, and that they have in relation to temporal effects the value of " common causes " in subordination to which the " proper causes " of these effects should normally be brought in action. " Oratio . . . summorum effectuum est causa propria et remedium proprium ; respectu inferiorum est causa communis." (Cajetan, de Auctor. papae, Tract. I. cap. 27.) On the other hand, the means of the second and of the third categories that we have marked out above have the value of " proper causes " in relation to temporal effects.

In the lowest rank we put secular means and in particular those means that fall under the general description of courage in attack. To exclude these means in principle would be tantamount to a denial that one had a body, and to imagine that the acts of the majority of men are dictated by reason. Coercion is for the foolish and the foolish outnumber the wise. If the modern world has sought to degrade and to dishonour force, as it has sought to degrade and dishonour reason, force and reason alike keep none the less their nature unimpaired ; and faith which has power to purify the uses to which we put reason and force is able also to restore their dignity. In certain special circumstances of political life (like those that have been mentioned above[1]) it will always be open to men of good faith to resort to force. To take a notable instance, in the existing condition of the world it is not possible to exclude from consideration the case of the accession to power of a usurper and of the measure of armed resistance that may be used against him.

It is possible, at least in theory—on the supposition of a successful effort of " authentic humanism " towards the reconstruction of the temporal régime, and of certain other rather improbable events—that, after a period of preparatory activity of greater or less duration, force would be needed for final achievement. Aggressive force and secular means of warfare would, however, be brought into operation as a secondary instrument in subordination to what we have called measures of organic reconstruction, and also to spiritual means of warfare the possible

[1] See pp. 153-4.

uses of which we have outlined. Purified in their
proper sphere by the prescriptions of justice and of
prudence, reduced maybe to the dimension of the
little sling of David in comparison with the great
engines of sin which are available to revolutions
that rely on such engines, the limitation and the
loss of power that follow from obedience to moral
rules would begin to be offset from the moment
aggressive and secular force ceased to be the sole
influences at work and fell back into the second line,
the preponderating power being then with spiritual
activity. At this point one may observe the essential
difference that separates endurance and suffering
voluntarily borne from what is called passive
resistance. The latter is a form of secular action
and is nothing more than the lowest and the weakest
expression of aggressive force ; while the activities
we have in mind belong to a different order as
Gandhi very properly pointed out a propos *Satyagraha*. One may also observe that the conflict
and the perplexity that arise out of the use of secular
means of warfare (as was pointed out on a previous
page) and that are mitigated by the general subordination of means of warfare to measures of
organic or moral reconstruction would be fully
resolved by the subordination of secular to spiritual
means.

Finally it is to be noted that if in political warfare
the first place were given to the temporal uses of
spiritual activity, a fundamental change would
follow in the attitude of the soul towards the course
of events and towards history. A soul that gave
pride of place to this kind of spiritual activity,

whose power is based on laws of the Providential order, would come to regard its proper action and the whole course of history as subordinate to a higher purpose. There is an element of presumption in wishing to precipitate things and to effect the Revolution—one's own revolution. The greatest men are apt to be deceived in it ; they always find at the finish that they have achieved something other than they had willed. One who works at his own post in the history which God makes through men and of which He alone knows the issue always does what he willed to do since it is not his own will that he wished to do. And he has a better sense of the value of time : and knows that in relation to the ends that he sets before him acts of violence matter less than measures of organic or moral reconstruction, and that sudden shifts are of less importance than the obscure changes they register and complete.

The Question of Fact

19. The philosopher is led to broach questions (most often thankless) of a practical kind by the sense of his responsibility towards souls, a sense which wins him no man's gratitude and of which even he realises the absurdity—for what forsooth is this pretended responsibility, seeing that no one listens ? In the long run his talk is for the angels.

It has thus been necessary to raise and to attempt to solve the question of the purification or spiritual preparation of the means of a renewal of the temporal order that shall be directed to the true well-being

of the commonwealth and to the freedom of autonomy
of individual citizens. It is scarcely necessary to add
that such a reform is likely in the present condition
of the world to meet with obstacles of a very special
kind. Even supposing that God should raise up
leaders with the capacity to carry the work through,
powerful forces would in any event rise up and
oppose it. In many countries political bodies
committed openly or covertly to a materialist ideal
have taken the lead and are using all the resources
of violence to bring about revolutions inspired by
imperial or dictatorial ideas of political life and
freedom. It is not impossible that on a future day
and for an appreciable time every means of activity
save purely spiritual activity may as in the first
centuries of the Church be closed to Christians.
On the other hand, in modern economic conditions
every transformation of the social order, although
it is in the first instance brought to pass within
such and such national frontiers, of its nature
claims to be applied to all peoples and, it seems,
can only be fully established if it is applied on a world-
wide scale : a situation that adds strangely to the
difficulties that surround a reconstruction of the
temporal order on a spiritual basis. A purely
objective view of things thus inclines one to the
opinion that the peace and balance and unity of the
temporal order to which the world aspires will
more probably be realised (in a precarious fashion,
leading in the end to catastrophe) in a style and by
means that are antichristian rather than in a style
and by means that are truly Christian.

While not failing to recognise that a renaissance

of the Christian spirit throughout the masses of the people is a real possibility in view of the means that are at the disposal of God and of the apostolic action of the saints who may arise among the masses (and for whom the world is calling), we have already indicated the very real obstacle that for the time being springs from the revolutionary materialism that is professed by so large a proportion of the working classes. Of those who favour a " revolution of the spirit " many are yet in search of a definite doctrine. Partly because the work of their elders was inadequate and partly because they are anxious to be under no obligation to the work of these elders, the inclination they follow seems to belong to the biological order, or to be that of a generation which wishes to try its luck with a new pack of cards ; a course that is surely legitimate but that implies a certain indifference to real spiritual values. A work of admirable intellectual and spiritual quality is being done among the younger generation but it is apt to be the achievement of individuals who have not learned to work together in a team.

These considerations are not of a kind to deter men from temporal activity. Even the greatest obstacles have never stopped but rather stimulated the action of men of faith. The temporal situation of France would not seem to have been any better in the time of Joan of Arc than is that of the world to-day. It is all the more important, therefore, to describe things as they really are.

It is possible that every attempt to transform the social régime along the lines of authentic humanism may fail, at least as far as outward appearances go.

In such a case those who love God would exercise an efficacious—though hidden—influence on the temporal by the use of " poor temporal means "[1] not in directly bringing about even a partial reconstruction of the social order, but by fidelity in thought and love and by the touch of faithful hands on the work of a faithless world.   Above all, in such a case, their office would be to bear witness to the spiritual order.   The labour of Anti-christ will be in vain. He goes before and announces Christ, even while striving against Him.   The rôles of Justice are played by the actors of iniquity.   The evolution of the universe and the acquisition of the forms and structures that are assigned to its final stage by Him Who made it may take place in the midst of a world in rebellion and under the banners of Blasphemy. The true significance of these things will appear only when the night of Time shall open on Eternity.

It is in the hour of Sorrows of the Messiah that His Kingdom will come, in a way that shall be invisible to the eyes of flesh and to the fallen spirits.

It is moreover to be observed that one who uses only secular means is disarmed when a stronger than he deprives him of his weapons.   But the Christian is never disarmed.   He expands or contracts his field of action according to the turns and changes of human history.   He is in the world yet not of the world.   No one can deprive him of the first and most important of the means he uses, for these means are of the spiritual order and make use of time without being consumed by it.

Not that his situation is comfortable or easy.

[1] See p. 133.

191

It never has been and is now so less than ever. More and more the Christian finds he must work at the peril of his soul. There is between the world and the soul a strange fellowship. The world suffers because of the state of souls ; souls suffer because of the state of the world. For is not the world in the soul by way of knowledge and of love, and is not the soul in the world by way of action and of passion ? They form worlds and wholes that interpenetrate each other and that even in the natural order (as Leibniz says) constitute an organic whole of which all the parts are related one to another and at the same time constitute a harmony. And the supernatural order again unites all souls that actually or virtually belong to it as dead or living members in the unity of another Body, which is endowed with a true mystical personality and whose task is to work out in time the redemption of that other body that is made up of the world and of the soul.

The world and the souls of men have entered into a period of darkness and of peril where the spirit of bewilderment and the other spirits of darkness of whom St. John of the Cross speaks may be expected to assail them. But the same Saint teaches that these long nights of agony are also periods of purification that lead those who know how to make use of them to life in its more perfect forms.

APPENDIX I

PERSON AND PROPERTY

No attempt is made in the following pages to deal at full length with the problem of property or to propound a new theory of the subject. On the contrary, our essay is based on the teaching of St. Thomas and his commentators which is assumed to be well-known.[1] We merely attempt, in brief and schematic form, to draw attention to certain fundamental principles in the metaphysic of human life and action which in our view are vital to the issue and which have not always been elucidated with sufficient care.

In the thought of St. Thomas, the theory of property presents three successive stages.

In the first stage he shows[2] that man considered in his specific nature has a general right of appro-

[1] The bibliography of the subject is very considerable, but we will refer only to the following : two essays by C. Spicq : *La Notion analogique de dominium et le droit de propriété* (Revue des sc. phil. et théol., 1931, pp. 52–76) and *Comment construire un traité thomiste de la propriété* (*Bull. thomiste*, July, 1931), and the book by A. Horváth, *Eigentumrecht nach dem hl. Thomas von Aquin* (Moser, Graz, 1929), which has recently been the subject of lively controversy. (Cf. *Bull. thomiste*, January, 1932 and July–October, 1932.)
Our point of view, moreover, is somewhat different from that of the classical exponents of the subject. Moral philosophy, a branch of knowledge which is speculatively practical, necessarily has its roots in metaphysics ; and the main object of this essay is to trace some of the roots that underlie the present problem.

[2] *Summa theol.*, II–II, 66, 1.

priation over all material things, the *vocation* of
these being to serve the needs of mankind, and their
appropriation by this or that man being thus the
fulfilment of a purpose which is inscribed in the
nature of things. The use (*usus*) which human
freedom makes of things appears then as the joint
act of freedom exercising its power and of things
fulfilling their natural destiny.

This is the capital truth which governs the whole
discussion and which shows that every person by
reason of his membership of the human species
ought in one way or another to derive advantage
from this common dedication of material things
to the good of the human race.

At the moment, however, we are not concerned
with the question of individual appropriation;
though it is this very question which presents most
difficulties.

In the second stage of his argument, St. Thomas
shows that the appropriation of external goods should
normally take place through individual ownership.
The rights of man over material goods imply in
fact the power to manage, administer and use these
goods (*potestas procurandi et dispensandi*)[1], which
power as a rule can be properly exercised only by
individual persons. In this way alone can one hope
to secure in the ordinary course the care that is
required in the management of goods, and the
absence of confusion, and the maintenance of the
public peace. It is thus " natural reason " which
establishes the rule of individual appropriation as
the rule of human possession of material things.[2]

[1] *Summa theol.*, II–II, 66, 2.   [2] *Ibid.*, II–II, 57, 3 ad 3.

" If a particular piece of land be considered in the absolute there is no reason why it should belong to one man rather than to another ; but if it be considered from the point of view of convenience of culture and peaceful use of the land, there is a certain fitness in allowing it to be the property of one man to the exclusion of all others."[1]

The use (*usus*) of these goods ought none the less to be common and of benefit to all by virtue of the common dedication of material goods which has been manifest from the beginning.

" With regard to external things, a man ought to possess them not as his own but as common, and always be ready to put them at the disposal of others who are in need."[2]

The third stage of the argument has to do with particular kinds of ownership. These are subject to evolution in the course of history. Neither legislation nor custom has any power to abolish the principle of private property, for this would involve a violation of natural law ; but they may regulate in different ways, according to the requirements of the common good, the exercise of the rights of ownership.[3]

Here we are concerned with the second of these three stages, viz. with the problem of individual appropriation in general without reference to particular kinds of ownership. Our object is to determine more precisely what are the elements in human nature on which the general right to own private property is founded ; or in other words to discover

[1] *Ibid.*, II–II, 57, 3.   [2] *Summa theol.*, II–II, 66, 2.
[3] Cf. *ibid.*, I–II, 95, 2 ; II Polit., Lectio IV.

what it is in human nature that calls for the individual appropriation of material goods.

This right will thus find a universal ground in a general postulate of human nature, independently of the particular *modes* or titles of acquiring property —such as occupation, succession, contract and the like—which will vary in individual circumstances and changing historical conditions : this, however, is outside our scope. The general postulate we are seeking follows in our view from the activity of man as maker—or as artist in the broad sense of the word—an activity which springs from the very essence of human personality.

1. PERSONA AND " FACTIBILE "

1. The activity of man in the present order is divided into " poetic " activity, or activity concerned with the making of things (which has for its object what the Schoolmen call the *factibile*, the thing to be made or produced) ; and ethical or moral activity which has for its object what the Schoolmen call the *agibile*, or acts to be done.

2. If we investigate the principles of Thomist philosophy the whole problem of personal appropriation appears to lie between two branches of an antinomy, between two extremes and apparently opposed affirmations. That which belongs to reason in operation, the *factibile*, requires individual appropriation ; that which on the contrary relates to the moral use of material goods demands that in one way or another such goods be at the service of all.

Man as artist is entitled to appropriate and to own ; man as moral agent is held to the ' common use ' of the things he has appropriated.

3.   Art is defined by the Schoolmen as *recta ratio factibilium*, the use of right reason in the making of things.   It is contrasted with prudence, *recta ratio agibilium*.[1]   We here use the word 'art' not in its strict sense and as divided into ' work ' and ' play,'[2] but in its more general meaning of intellectual activity that has to do with the production of a work or the elaboration of material as opposed to moral activity which has to do with the exercise of free will.

Here is the metaphysical element in human nature which in a general way makes personal ownership a matter of necessity and which is the ground of proprietary right.[3]

Such work may not be ' artistic ' in the ordinary sense of the word but it is always artistic in the broad sense in which we use it here.   It always involves application of human reason to the elaboration of some material, and it thus belongs always to the order of *factibile* and is accordingly connected with the metaphysical ground of ownership. The principle holds good whether the work be that of a craftsman or a manual labourer.

[1] Cf. *Art and Scholasticism*, Chapter IV, note 4.
[2] Cf. Etienne Borne, *Travail et Esprit chrétien*, Courrier des Iles, No. I, 1932.
[3] This is a different thing from work viewed as a title to property (" even as the effect follows the cause so is it just that the fruits of the work should belong to the worker," Leo XIII, *Rerum Novarum*), although the title to property created by work is an application and a determination under very variable forms of this metaphysical principle.

4. We maintain that the exercise of art or work is the formal reason of individual appropriation; but only because it presupposes the rational nature and personality of the artist or workman.

In the case of the bee, for instance, or of the beaver there is no exercise of art or of work in the strict sense (since there is no *reason* in operation); neither is there any individual ownership.

The notion of ' person ' must thererore be included in any complete theory of property, since the *persona* is the proper subject of intellect in operation.

5. In the ontological and immanent order each person possesses a proprietary right over himself, over his nature and his action; a mastery over himself, and over his acts. So in the theological order the Person of the Word possesses his human nature as proper to him. This is in the metaphysical order the root principle of individual ownership,[1] but it can only pass to ownership of material and external goods by way of the *factibile*, the exercise of art or work.

It is of the very essence of this activity to imprint on matter the mark of rational being. Now by virtue of what the work of art or the work to be done demands for its proper perfection it is in the nature of things necessary that man shall have the fullest control over the material on which he has to work, that the master-craftsman shall have permanent and exclusive right of disposal of the material and of the means necessary for executing the work.

[1] The views on *dominium* put forward by the Rev. Fr. Spicq are particularly relevant in this connection. Article quoted above, p. 193, note (i).

But this can only be realised through a general system of individual ownership (whatever be the modes, more or less felicitous, in which the system takes shape) even though there may be workers who do not own the instruments of their work—the wage-earners—and though there be also work (*factibilia*) which owing to special circumstances lies outside the scope of private management, as for instance the public services of the State or undertakings which come under its control.

In the first case the *wage-earner* is considered as ' member ' of another man whom he *serves* and whose practical reason regulates and determines in the first place the work that is to be done. And in his character as *means or instrument of another person* the wage-earner is neither owner nor co-owner of the concern. Even so the dignity which is proper to him as a *person*, as one who works up material and is master of it, is not abolished. By virtue of this dignity, the individual appropriation radically required by the *factibile* still operates for him on the side of the *product*, that is the profits, for which the fixed wage is a substitute.

In the second case the work of the *official* is grafted on free work and presupposes it. It is in the nature of things that such work should be exceptional and limited to what directly concerns the common good of the community.

6. Through the *factible*—the exercise of art or work—the proprietorship that the person has over himself is thus extended to the ownership of things. How does this come about? Through those

199

internal qualities which the Schoolmen call *habitus* (ἕξεις), stable dispositions that perfect the subject, especially in the field of action.

The ' artistic ' work (we use the word ' artistic ' equivocally) of the bee proceeds from its specific nature ; but the artistic and productive work of man is the outcome of personal activity and of the *habitus* of each. The very word *habitus* is significant : one *has* what the other has not.

This is why the work of art or the thing to be made, the *factibile* which proceeds from the *habitus*, requires the personal power of management and use (*potestas procurandi et dispensandi*) of which St. Thomas speaks. It requires that things, materials, and means of work be possessed by man as a personal right, in lasting and permanent possession that befits an agent who has foresight and intelligence and whose judgment and action are taken with eyes wide open to the future. In short the material that is to be wrought needs to be the property of him who works on it, of the rational being who operates on it—a rational being which is individual and which has an individual perfection.[1]

The master man, moreover, who plans out the work, is also normally the head of a family who

---

[1] One can understand that through an illusion proper to it machinery (if one overlooks the wealth of artistic capital that it uses) appears to destroy the right to property by inducing the belief that human life can do without personal *habitus* and operative intellectual virtues, all the necessary work on raw material being assured by a world of automatons, as if the manufacture of machines and their control, far from taking the place of art did not simply shift its ground and carry it (so to say) to the next power.

makes provision for his children. The work he performs is directed not merely to his own needs but primarily to the needs of the community of which he is the head. There is thus a close relationship between personal property and the family viewed as the primeval unit of society antecedent to the State.[1]

To prevent external things from becoming the *things* of the family (capable of hereditary transmission in various modes to members of the family) is to destroy the material basis of the family. The truth of this becomes evident if we consider the head of the family as ' workman ' or *artifex*—as the mind in operation in the making of things.

If on the other hand civil life implies mutual intercourse which takes place through the will of private individuals and thus witnesses in social life to individual liberty of action and presupposes the private possession of things which individual citizens can of their own authority part with by purchase, sale, gift[2] and so on, these things are so because individual citizens are the subjects of intellectual operation and because they have the power to impose a rational elaboration on material things.

7. The metaphysical foundation of private property has thus to do with the artistic side of human nature. The vocation of human nature to elaborate raw material according to a rational design requires

---

[1] " Immo tanto jus est illud (dominii) validius, quanto persona humana in convictu domestico plura complectitur." Leo XIII, *Rerum Novarum.*
[2] *Summa theol.*, I–II, 105, 2.

generally that external things on which and by which this elaboration is wrought should be possessed as of right by the person whose rational activity is in operation. Here is the metaphysical root of the two fundamental titles to individual property, namely occupation (the first occupier laying hold of certain goods with a view to their later elaboration) and work.

8. These foundations are based on right and are of universal application. Because of the disorder that is inherent in human affairs, it rarely happens in fact that the best practical intellect possesses goods which correspond to its *habitus*. Herein lies disorder. But a certain disorder is inherent in the very existence of human things ; and what we are now seeking is the general foundation of property right which shall answer once and for all the needs of human personality, and not those special conditions with which separate individuals must comply in order to become lawful owners of specific goods.

9. One may say, however, that a society will be more perfect in proportion as technical competence and effective work go hand in hand with ownership.

When the anarchy to which we have referred passes a certain limit, and more particularly when super-individual groups and interests acting irresponsibly and without rational direction impose *their* disorder on the administration of material goods, and in point of fact (under a régime too which is based on private property) take precedence over technicians and workmen—a revolution in the social body is inevitable.

10.   Finally the State and just laws may intervene not for the purpose of depriving the citizens of their right to own property, but to regulate the exercise of this right and to order it to the common good. The exercise of the right may even be suspended in certain extreme cases, as for example when persons refuse to develop the goods they possess (*latifundia*) or choose to destroy instead of developing them.

11.   The modes of individual ownership normally correspond to the work to be done (*factibile*) and the exercise of art and work. Work done on the soil, even if mechanical processes are used, is typically adapted to the work of a family group, to the art which the head of the family possesses, and which he can exercise with the help of the members of the domestic circle. This circle can be extended to comprise a greater or lesser number of associated co-workers or wage-earners. Such work tends as a matter of course towards the *family* type of ownership.

On the other hand the industrial method of production, particularly in the manufacturing industries, passes beyond the normal sphere of family co-operation as it is found among agricultural labourers or artisans. This mode of production is typically adapted to the art and work of a kind of community or technical society the leaders of which are so to speak the political leaders of the *factibile*. It tends as a matter of course towards a *corporate* type of ownership, namely co-ownership. In fact we have to do at the present time with a swarm of shareholders with technicians and workmen in their service. The salary of the technician and of the workman is a substitute (eliminating any share of risk) for what his profit would be as co-owner of the concern and from the product of the undertaking. This system has given rise to such serious abuses that normal administration would seem to require us to return to a type of industrial ownership in which a group of technicians, workers, and sleeping partners would all be co-owners of the concern.

II. " USUS " AND COMMON USE

12. The thesis of St. Thomas is that the use of things (*usus*) must in some sense be common ; must, that is, be of service to all. We may with profit refer to the technical meaning which St. Thomas attaches to the notion of *use* when speaking of *usus activus* in his analysis of human acts.[1]

" The use of any thing implies the application of that thing to some operation : hence the operation to which we apply a thing is called its use ; thus to ride is to use a horse[2] and to strike is to use a stick."

St. Thomas also adds that we bring to the operation the interior powers of the soul, the members of the body and external things " sicut baculum ad percutiendum." Here is the *usus* which we have to study. It is an act of free exercise of the will. We no longer have to do with the order of the *factibile*

---

[1] Cf. *Summa theol.*, I–II, q. 16.
[2] But though *equitare* is *usus equi, ditari* is not *usus divitiarum*. This might serve indeed as the very formula of Capitalist deviation.

or the exercise of art and work ; it is the order of the *agibile*, namely the moral law which now comes into play. Take the example of the stick ; there is a technique in the procuring of it and in the wielding of it. But the wielding of the stick, which is an art from the point of view of the *factibile*, is also a moral act from the point of view of *usus*. Thus the administration of *my* goods, which, in the line of the *factibile*, is a technique personally exercised by me, is also a moral act (*usus*) which, as such, must somehow regard the good of all—in the first place my own good of course, but my good as a member of the community.

In article 2 of the same question (16) St. Thomas teaches that *usus* does not belong to irrational animals because it implies free will. In article 3 he shows that we cannot *use* the last end ; we enjoy the end, but means—useful things—we use. Finally in article 4 he explains how use follows choice. Choice is the last moment of the will in free relation of affective union and interior adjustment to the thing willed. Yet after choice has been made there is what we may call another wave of will : it is the *usus* which constitutes the last moment of the will as it tends to a *real union ;* to a *real* grasp of the means it has chosen.

13. Use must be in some sense common. " In respect of use man ought to possess external things, not as his own but as common."[1]

---

[1] " Unde manifestum est quod multo melius est quod sint propriae possessiones secundum dominium, *sed quod fiant communes aliquo modo quantum ad usum.*" St. Thomas, *Comm. in Polit. Aristotelis*, lib. II, Lect. IV—Cf. *Summa theol.*, II–II, 32, 5, ad 2 ; 66, 2.

This law derives in the first place from the prime universal purpose of material goods. The dedication of earthly goods not to individual men but to man, to humankind, always holds good and rules all else, since it is original and the ground of the very right to possess material things, before we come to titles of individual ownership of these things.

In the second place (it is really another aspect of the same argument) the law which requires that the *usus* or benefit of material goods shall be common may be deduced from the nature of *usus* as such. The *usus* bears directly on *means* and in relation to them it is the last act of the will directing the faculties to real union and possession. It is the final act of moral freedom in relation to *means* or things in use.

The act itself is mine : it is personal, but the relation of this act to external things gives me no right to own them ; the act presupposes the right. It would only confer the right if I were personally the object and end of this utility ; if it were by nature destined for me, which is not the case since its natural destiny is to man in general ; or if the fact of freely relating a good to myself as end, to my natural love of self, sufficed to give me a right to this good, which equally is not the case.

And indeed if we consider exclusively the aspect of the *agibile*, or the situation of moral acts in the movement of man towards his last end, there seems no reason (each person being an entity in relation to the rest of the world) why one person more than another should have the use of the goods of this world.

Thus from the point of view of *usus*, of the moral use of external goods, it is not individual appropriation which is established, but the common destination of goods which must be achieved in one way or another. And this ordering of things to the service of all should exist by universal rule and not be confined to the case in which it takes material shape in the surrender (which I am morally bound to make)[1] of my surplus to the common use.

In every human act that has to do with external goods, these two aspects of *factibile* and *agibile*, of operation and moral use, appear. The one and the other, individual appropriation and common use, should shine forth in every act which concerns external goods.

Such use may be an act of my will directing my faculties to enjoy a material good, in the way of consumption or of spending, in eating fruit for example, or in spending my wages in the purchase of the *Critique of Pure Reason*. There is use and individual enjoyment of the fruit and of the wage and of the book ; and even here in the enjoyment itself the metaphysical origin of private ownership is found in the claims of the *factibile ;* for my bodily or intellectual mechanism must be maintained. But, we may ask, is there any trace here of the law which requires that use should be common ? It appears in the fact that this mechanism must itself serve the common good. And if my act is governed by reason not by greed it is implicitly ordered to the common good without any necessity for conscious thought on my part.

[1] Cf. *Summa theol.*, II–II, 32, 5 ; 66, 7.

14. From these observations certain important consequences may be deduced, which fall under these three headings :—

(1) Every use of goods which is not regulated by reason is an act of *avarice* which deprives others of their due. This applies to things necessary as well as to things superfluous ; for in every use of material goods which is governed not by reason but by selfish indulgence there is sin not only against God and myself but also against my neighbour. I am never alone in any one of my acts. The poor are always with us everywhere claiming their right.

(2) The law of ' common use ' obviously bears on *utilisation* and on the *fructus*, the enjoyment of things. This may be realised in two ways which were foreseen under the Old Law,[1] either through the enjoyment of certain goods being actually in common or shared amongst all ; or through the interchange of goods at the will of their owners, by way of gift, sale, purchase, loan, hiring, deposit, and so forth. But the law of ' common use ' also has relation to the *cura*, the administration of goods.[2] In one view, so far as it is a matter of *usus*[3] and not of technique, the administration of goods means their dedication to the common weal.

The acquisition and consumption or use I make of my goods (which belong as such to the province of art or of technique) as a responsible owner must be governed by the requirements of right user and must serve the common good and advantage.

---

[1] *Summa theol.*, I–II, 105, 2.   [2] *Ibid.*
[3] See above, p. 205.

The law may intervene here, even prior to the consideration of what is superfluous and before any distinction is made between what is necessary and what is superfluous. [1] We are not here concerned with the question whether the owner of goods is bound to give away some of the things that are necessary or things that are surplus. We are emphasizing the necessity of an *organisation*—a social structure—which will ensure a certain measure of enjoyment (*fructus*) for all and also a certain administrative responsibility (*cura*) in all.

One can see that the requirement of moral user (*usus*) may have a repercussion on management and administration, on *cura* and even on *procuratio*. Even now in countries established on the basis of private ownership there are to be found many instances of industrial undertakings in which the workers share in the management although they are not yet regarded as co-owners of the undertaking but only as wage-earners. [2]

(3) Only now do we need to consider questions as to surplus goods and the duty of devoting them to the common good. Such questions are rather for the individual conscience or the confessional than for sociology or legislation. The laws that affect the matter (sumptuary laws, income tax, etc.) normally make up only for deficiencies in individual virtue. They are therefore quite inadequate for

[1] Cf. St. Thomas, *in Polit.*, lib. II, lect. IV : " Quomodo autem usus rerum propriarum possit fieri communis, hoc pertinet ad providentiam boni legislatoris."

[2] Compare particularly the experiments at Glenwood carried out by the American Baltimore and Ohio Company (H. Dubreuil, *Standards*, Paris, 1929, pp. 367 sq. ; Otto S. Beyer, *Bulletin of the Taylor Society*, February, 1926).

the proper organisation of *usus communis ;* whereas in the matters indicated under the previous sub-division the law is fulfilling its primary and proper function.

If we limit our consideration to what is necessary and what is superfluous, and allow the principle of *usus communis* to operate only in such cases, our view of the problem will be narrow and ineffectual.

We must not forget that justice provides only for a minimum. The claims of ' common use ' are much wider ; and require friendship as well as justice in the structure of the city.

15. When the ' common use ' of goods falls below a certain limit, a revolution in the social body is inevitable.

The measure of ' common use,' the manner in which the goods of each fulfil the obligation to be of advantage to all, follows the measure of individual and social morality. It must therefore be safe-guarded by the " just laws and good customs " to which Aristotle and St. Thomas alike refer.

It would seem that the disorder in modern society has reached an acute stage. Individual owner-ship has declined greatly on the side of operative reason, just where it is postulated by the needs of work and ' artistic ' activity (in the line of the *factibile*) ; while on the side of the moral reason there is a sharp decline in the sharing of individual ownership, just where it is postulated by the necessities of moral action (in other words in the line of the *agibile*). The evident requirements of modern legislation do no more in reality than secure a strict minimum by way of compensation for the absence of a spontaneous ' common use.'

16. It might be said that in the same degree in which art is inhuman, so likewise is property ; but, like art, property corresponds to a deep need in human nature. Art, in the widest sense of the word, and ownership belong rather to the intellectual side of human nature (the practical intellect).

' Use,' on the other hand, with its obligation to be of service to all, belongs rather to the will and moral life. One sees why it is that moral (humanitarian) reasons are used against ownership ; whereas technical and intellectual (utilitarian) reasons are used in its favour.

Communism is especially open to criticism on the ethical plane in relation to the law of ' common use,' which can only be inadequately safeguarded by the State, its spiritual foundation resting in the last resort on human personality and on love. No social organisation however necessary it may be in other respects for enforcing the principle of ' common use ' can take the place of the most human mode of sharing goods, which is the way of friendship. If this principle is to prevail in the State, there must be a spiritual basis for the social structure and a general respect for the life of the soul and human personality.

On the other hand it is on the intellectual (or artistic) plane that communism is open to criticism from the side of the *factibile* and of the requirements of human activity in the rational elaboration of material. Individual ownership of material goods is based on a spiritual foundation, on the capacity of the rational being as an intellectual subject to give form to matter.

In the sphere of purely material production, particularly in industry, communism can temporarily at least and by the use of tyranny exalt the operative activity of human reason. But such activity can only be hindered or corrupted by communism in the sphere where the activity of human reason is of the highest civilising influence ; on the plane where art like pure speculation is held captive by the vision of something in the transcendental order which it seeks to represent or to contemplate.

17. We say that in the sphere of purely material production and for a time, communism can exalt operative activity but by the use of tyranny and not otherwise. We may recall that according to St. Thomas[1] the three principal conditions which distinguish good work in a community are carefulness in the administration of goods, absence of confusion in the work done, and maintenance of the public peace. If in fact such conditions can only be realised under a régime based on the private owner-ship of material goods, it is because their existence is commensurate with a really stable and human order worthy of the dignity of the person, which means that they come into being *naturally and freely* if the organisation of society (which is itself a product of reason) fulfils and does not destroy the spontaneity of nature or the free play of human activity.

When a régime based on private property becomes

[1] *Summa theol.*, II-II, 66, 2. See above, p. 195.

depersonalized and passes in actual fact under the sway of inorganic collective forces, the advantages we have cited disappear, as is evident in our day.

On the other hand, where coercion on the part of the community has been able in some measure to take the place of a natural and spontaneous order the same advantages may be secured in a collectivist society, but in an artificial and tyrannical fashion. In this way alone can a communist economic system function successfully. If the individual is careful in the administration of his goods it is no longer because of his responsibility for the work itself, or for the thing which is no longer his ; consequently neither success nor failure affects or even interests him directly. The reason for his solicitude lies in his responsibility towards the community whose servant he is ; towards other men who will punish him if he fails in his duty. If the work is carried through without disorder or confusion in the social body, and if public peace is secured, it is due to the iron discipline imposed on the individual by the community, and on the workers by those who direct the work and whose reason supplies the rule according to which the work must be done.

18. Here then is the reason why communism is led to postulate a radical change in human nature. The inducements to work, and to good work, are no longer to be looked for in the private interests of the individual. (And, be it noted, the bourgeois world had degraded these interests to the lowest level ; for they are not necessarily either selfish or servile or bound up with the desire to accumulate

endless wealth.) The communist zeal for work, on the contrary, must spring from a pure and mystical devotion to the community and from a paradisial joy in work itself. Man is led to attain to this happy state by flogging and the dread of starvation ; his imagination is enslaved to the various myths of propaganda. Here, in the need to change the nature of man and to convert him into a slave who will joyfully shed his personality and surrender himself to the collective task is the material explanation of the effort that communism is making to change man by turning him into an atheist. For God is the supreme and overmastering interest of human personality.

APPENDIX II

THE DOCTRINE OF " SATYAGRAHA " AS SET FORTH BY M. K. GANDHI

The Report of the Commissioners appointed by the Punjab Sub-Committee of the Indian National Congress, 1920, Vol. I, Chapter 4, gives an account of " *Satyagraha*. In this is included a special note by Mr. Gandhi himself, who sets forth " his social doctrine known as *Satyagraha*, a civic claim for truth, a weapon of popular action and of high moral value, which may perhaps outlast the political circumstances in which its author conceived it." (Louis Massignon, *Revue du Monde Musulman*, April-June, 1921.) The following is an extract from the Report mentioned, Vol. I, Chapter 4 :—

" For the past thirty years I have been preaching and practising *Satyagraha*. The principles of *Satyagraha*, as I know it to-day, constitute a gradual evolution.

" The term *Satyagraha* was coined by me in South Africa to express the force that the Indians there used for full eight years, and it was coined in order to distinguish it from the movement, then going on in the United Kingdom and South Africa under the name of Passive Resistance.

" Its root meaning is ' holding on to truth '; hence, Truth-force. I have also called it Love-force or Soul-force. In the application of *Satyagraha* I discovered in the earliest stages that pursuit of truth did not admit of violence being inflicted on one's opponent, but that he must be weaned from error by patience and sympathy. For what appears to be truth to the one may appear to be error to the other. And patience means self-suffering. So the doctrine came to mean vindication of truth, not by infliction of suffering on the opponent, but one's own self.

" *Satyagraha* differs from Passive Resistance as the North Pole from the South. The latter has been conceived as a weapon of the weak and does not exclude the use of physical force or violence for the purpose of gaining one's end ; whereas the former has been conceived as a weapon of the strongest, and excludes the use of violence in any shape or form.

" When Daniel disregarded the laws of the Medes and Persians which offended his conscience, and meekly suffered the punishment for his disobedience, he offered *Satyagraha* in its purest form. Socrates would not refrain from preaching what he knew to be the truth to the Athenian youth, and bravely suffered the punishment of death. He was, in this case, a *Satyagrahi*. Prahlad disregarded the orders of his father, because he considered them to be repugnant to his conscience. He uncomplainingly and cheerfully bore the tortures, to which he was subjected, at the instance of his father. Mirabai, who is said to have offended her husband by following her own conscience, was content to live in separation from him and bore with quiet dignity and resignation all the injuries that are said to have been done to her in order to bend her to her husband's will. Both Prahlad and Mirabai practised *Satya-graha*. It must be remembered that neither Daniel nor Socrates, neither Prahlad nor Mirabai had any ill-will towards their persecutors. Daniel and Socrates are regarded as having been model citizens of the States to which they belonged, Prahlad a model son, Mirabai a model wife.

" This doctrine of *Satyagraha* is not new ; it is merely an extension of the rule of domestic life to the political. Family disputes and differences are generally settled according to the law of love. The injured member has so much regard for the others that he suffers injury for the sake of his principles without retaliating and without being angry with those who differ from him. And as repression of anger and self-suffering are difficult processes, he does not dignify trifles into principles, but, in all non-essentials, readily agrees with the rest of the family, and thus contrives to gain the maximum of peace for himself without disturbing that of the others. Thus his action, whether he resists or resigns, is always calculated to promote the common welfare of the family. It is this law of love which, silently but surely, governs the family for the most part throughout the civilized world.

" I feel that nations cannot be one in reality, nor can their activities be conducive to the common good of the whole humanity, unless there is this definite recognition and acceptance of the law of the family in national and international affairs, in other words, on the political platform. Nations can be called civilized, only to the extent that they obey this law.

" This law of love is nothing but a law of truth. Without truth there is no love ; without truth it may be affection, as for one's country to the injury of others ; or infatuation, as of a young man for a girl ; or love may be unreasoning and blind, as of ignorant parents for their children. Love transcends all animality and is never partial. *Satyagraha* has therefore been described as a coin, on whose face you read love and on the reverse you read truth. It is a coin current everywhere and has indefinable value.

" *Satyagraha* is self-dependent. It does not require the assent of the opponent before it can be brought into play. Indeed it shines out most when the opponent resists. It is therefore irresistible. A *Satyagrahi* does not know what defeat is, for he fights for truth without being exhausted. Death in the fight is a deliverance, and prison a gateway to liberty.

" It is called also soul-force, because a definite recognition of the soul within is a necessity, if a *Satyagrahi* is to believe that death does not mean cessation of the struggle, but a culmination. The body is merely a vehicle for self-expression ; and he gladly gives up the body, when its existence is an obstruction in the way of the opponent seeing the truth, for which the *Satyagrahi* stands. He gives up the body in the certain faith that if anything would change his opponent's view, a willing sacrifice of his body must do so. And with the knowledge that the soul survives the body, he is not impatient to see the triumph of truth in the present body. Indeed, victory lies in the ability to die in the attempt to make the opponent see the truth, which the *Satyagrahi* for the time being expresses.

" And as a *Satyagrahi* never injures his opponent and always appeals, either to his reason by gentle argument or his heart by the sacrifice of self, *Satyagraha* is twice blessed, it blesses him who practises it, and him against whom it is practised.

" It has however been objected that *Satyagraha*, as we conceive it, can be practised only by a select few. My experience proves the contrary. Once its simple principles—adherence to truth and insistence upon it by self-suffering—are understood, anybody can practise it. It is as difficult or as easy to practise as any other virtue. It is as little necessary for its practice that everyone should understand the whole philosophy of it, as it is for the practice of total abstinence.

" After all, no one disputes the necessity of insisting on truth as one sees it. And it is easy enough to understand that it is vulgar to attempt to compel the opponent to its acceptance by using brute force ; it is discreditable to submit to error, because argument has failed to convince, and that the only true and honourable course is not to submit to it even at the cost of one's life. Then only can the world be purged of error, if it ever can be altogether. There can be no compromise with error where it hurts the vital being.

" But, on the political field, the struggle on behalf of the people mostly consists in opposing error in the shape of unjust laws. When you have failed to bring the error home to the law-giver by way of petitions and the like, the only remedy open to you, if you do not wish to submit to it, is to compel him to retrace his steps by suffering in your own person, i.e., by inviting the penalty for the breach of the law. Hence, *Satyagraha* largely appears to the public as civil disobedience or civil resistance. It is civil in the sense that it is not criminal.

" The criminal, i.e., the ordinary law-breaker, breaks the law surreptitiously and tries to avoid the penalty ; not so the civil resister. He ever obeys the laws of the state to which he belongs, not out of fear of the sanctions, but because he considers them to be good for the welfare of society. But there come occasions, generally rare, when he considers certain laws to be so unjust as to render obedience to them a dishonour; he then openly and civilly breaks them and quietly suffers the penalty for their breach. And in order to register his protest against the action of the law-giver, it is open to him to withdraw his co-operation from the state by dis-obeying such other laws whose breach does not involve moral turpitude. In my opinion, the beauty and efficacy of *Satyagraha* are so great and the doctrine so simple that it can be preached even to children. It was preached by me to thousands of men, women and children, commonly called indentured Indians, with excellent results.

" When the Rowlatt Bills were published, I felt that they were so restrictive of human liberty that they must be resisted to the utmost. I observed, too, that the opposition to them was universal among Indians. I submit that no state, however despotic, has the right to enact laws which are repugnant to the whole body of the people, much less a Government guided by constitutional usage and precedent, such as the Indian Government. I felt, too, that the oncoming agitation needed a definite direction, if it was neither to collapse nor to run into violent channels.

" I ventured therefore to present *Satyagraha* to the country, emphasizing its civil resistance aspect. And as it is purely an inward and purifying movement, I suggested the observance of fast, prayer and suspension of all work for one day—the 6th of April. There was a magnificent response throughout the length and breadth of India, even in little villages, although there was no organization and no great previous preparation. The idea was given to the public as soon as it was conceived. On the 6th April, there was no violence used by the people, and no collision with the police worth naming. The *Hartal* was purely voluntary and spontaneous. I took no steps to further the idea beyond publishing the following message on the 24th March last at Madras :—

" ' *Satyagraha*, as I have endeavoured to explain at several meetings, is essentially a religious move- ment. It is a process of purification and penance. It seeks to secure reforms or redress of grievances by self-suffering. I therefore venture to suggest that the second Sunday after the publication of the Viceregal assent to Bill No. 2 of 1919 (i.e., 6th April) may be observed as a day of humiliation and prayer. As there must be an effective public demonstration in keeping with the character of the observance, I beg to advise as follows :—

(i) A twenty-four hours' fast, counting from the last meal on the preceding night, should be observed by all adults, unless prevented from so doing by considerations of religion or health. The fast is not to be regarded, in any shape or form, in the nature of a hunger-strike, or as designed to put any pressure upon the Government. It is to be regarded for the *Satyagrahis* as a necessary discipline to fit them for civil disobedience, contemplated in their pledge, and for all others as some slight token of the intensity of their wounded feelings.

(ii) All work, except such as may be necessary in the public interest, should be suspended for the day. Markets and other business places should be closed. Employees who are required to work even on Sundays may only suspend work after obtaining previous leave.

" ' I do not hesitate to recommend these two suggestions for adoption by public servants. For though it is unquestionably the right thing for them not to take part in political discussion and gatherings, in my opinion they have an undoubted right to express, upon vital matters, their feelings in the very limited manner herein suggested.

(iii) Public meetings should be held on that day in all parts of India, not excluding villages, at which resolutions praying for the withdrawal of the two measures should be passed.

" ' If my advice is deemed worthy of acceptance

the responsibility will lie, in the first instance, on the various *Satyagraha* Associations for under-taking the necessary work of organization, but all other Associations will, I hope, join hands in making this demonstration a success.' "

SATYAGRAHA PLEDGE

" Being Conscientiously of opinion that the Bills known as the Indian Criminal Law (Amendment) Bill, No. 1 of 1919, and the Criminal Law (Emer-gency Powers) Bill, No. 2 of 1919, are unjust, sub-versive of the principles of liberty and justice, and destructive of the elementary rights of individuals on which the safety of the community, as a whole, and the State itself, is based, we solemnly affirm that, in the event of these Bills becoming law and until they are withdrawn, we shall refuse civilly to obey these laws and such other laws as a Committee to be hereafter appointed may think fit, and we further affirm that in this struggle we will faithfully follow truth and refrain from violence to life, person or property."